547289

815

Thonssen, Lester
    Representative American speeches: 1967-1968.
Wilson, 1968.
    218p (The reference shelf v40, no.5)
$3.00

DISCARD

    1. American orations. 2. Speeches,
addresses, etc. I. T $

                              38-27962

THE REFERENCE SHELF   VOLUME 40 NUMBER 5

REPRESENTATIVE AMERICAN SPEECHES: 1967-1968

EDITED BY LESTER THONSSEN

Professor of Speech
Metropolitan State College of Colorado at Denver

REPRESENTATIVE AMERICAN SPEECHES: 1967-1968

Copyright © 1968

By The H. W. Wilson Company

Library of Congress Catalog Card No. (30-23262)

THE H. W. WILSON COMPANY
NEW YORK   1968

THE REFERENCE SHELF

The books in this series contain reprints of articles, excerpts from books, and addresses on current issues and social trends in the United States and other countries. There are six separately bound numbers in each volume, all of which are generally published in the same calendar year. One number is a collection of recent speeches; each of the others is devoted to a single subject and gives background information and discussion from various points of view, concluding with a comprehensive bibliography.

Subscribers to the current volume receive the books as issued. The subscription rate is $14 in the United States and Canada ($17 foreign) for a volume of six numbers. Single numbers are $3.50 each in the United States and Canada ($4 foreign).

REPRESENTATIVE AMERICAN SPEECHES: 1967-1968
Copyright © 1968
By The H. W. Wilson Company
Library of Congress Catalog Card No. (38-27962)

PRINTED IN THE UNITED STATES OF AMERICA

PREFACE

Several years ago, an uncommonly snide trick was played on some unsuspecting members of the animal kingdom. A day-long festival was held commemorating the one hundredth anniversary of the development of the Rhode Island Red chicken. There were speeches memorializing the hen; a plaque to the hapless creature was dedicated; and the Rhode Island Red was singled out for its contribution to the multibillion dollar poultry industry.

After the kind words were spoken, do you know what the audience did? You are quite right. It ate one hundred Rhode Island Reds at a festive barbecue. A cynical gratitude, it would seem, with a bit of reverse English.

Yet it is not unlike the practice of some anthologists and critics who, with academic fanfare, select so-called great speeches or other creative expressions for special remembrance, and then promptly tear them to pieces with such cavalier delight as to make the readers wonder why they were chosen to begin with. This is not, however, a censure of the practice. Much good comes from it, for in the process of selection the critic often compares his choices with other addresses, thereby sharpening the focus of scrutiny on the distinctive features of the speakers. In private life, personal comparisons may indeed be odious; but comparative analyses of rhetorical practices need not be. A comparison of Ralph Waldo Emerson's and Wendell Phillips' calls for intellectual independence, for example, throws light upon both men, each in his own realm. And no offense arises from the admission that they argue differently. One can appreciate both, without chewing up and devouring either.

In his delightfully abrasive manner, H. L. Mencken once remarked that, by comparison with the famous rhetoricians he had heard, William Jennings Bryan was the greatest of

3

them all. His argument, "three times out of four," said Mencken, "was idiotic, but it at least hung together." Let us examine briefly—and I trust not too superficially—an example which illustrates how comparative estimates have been used to analyze an aspect of rhetorical effectiveness, namely, an orator's "sense of organization," his talent for making arguments hold together and reveal believable intellectual form. In his essay "Daniel Webster as a Master of English Style," the nineteenth-century critic Edwin P. Whipple wrote:

An ingenious and powerful, but paradoxical thinker, once told me that I was mistaken in calling Jonathan Edwards and Daniel Webster great reasoners. "They were bad reasoners," he added, "but great poets." Without questioning the right of the author of "An Enquiry into the Modern Prevailing Notion of That Freedom of Will, Which Is Supposed to Be Essential to Moral Agency," to be ranked among the most eminent of modern logicians, I could still understand why he was classed among poets; for whether Edwards paints the torments of hell or the bliss of heaven, his imagination almost rivals that of Dante in intensity of realization. But it was at first puzzling to comprehend why Webster should be depressed as a reasoner in order to be exalted as a poet. The images and metaphors scattered over his speeches are so evidently brought in to illustrate and enforce his statements and arguments, that, grand as they often are, the imagination displayed in them is still a faculty strictly subsidiary to the reasoning power. It was only after reflecting patiently for some time on the seeming paradox that I caught a glimpse of my friend's meaning; and it led me at once to consider an entirely novel question, not heretofore mooted by any of Webster's critics, whether friendly or unfriendly, in their endeavors to explain the reason of his influence over the best minds of the generation to which he belonged. In declaring that, as a poet, he far exceeded any capacity he evinced as a reasoner, my paradoxical friend must have meant that Webster had the poet's power of so *organizing* a speech, that it stood out to the eye of the mind as a palpable intellectual product and fact, possessing, not merely that vague reality which comes from erecting a plausible mental structure of deductive argumentation, based on strictly limited premises, but a positive reality, akin to the products of Nature herself, when she tries her hand in constructing a ledge of rocks or rearing a chain of hills. . . .

Now when a man, in whatever department or direction of thought his activity is engaged, succeeds in organizing, or even welding together, the materials on which he works, so that the product, as a whole, is *visible* to the mental eye, as a new creation or construction, he has an immense advantage over all critics of his performance. Refined reasonings are impotent to overthrow it; epigrams glance off from it, as rifle-bullets rebound when aimed at a granite wall; and it stands erect long after the reasonings and the epigrams are forgotten. . . . "The Reply to Hayne," "The Constitution Not a Compact Between Sovereign States," "The President's Protest," and others that might be mentioned, we shall find that they partake of the character of organic formations, or at least of skillful engineering or architectural constructions. Even Mr. Calhoun never approached him in this art of giving objective reality to a speech, which, after all, is found, on analysis, to consist only of a happy collocation and combination of words; but in Webster the words are either all alive with the creative spirit of the poet, or, at the worst, resemble the blocks of granite or marble which the artisan piles, one on the other, and the result of which, though it may represent a poor style of architecture, is still a rude specimen of a Gothic edifice. . . .

Is this power of organization common among orators? It seems to me that, on the contrary, it is very rare. In some of Burke's speeches, in which his sensibility and imagination were thoroughly under the control of his judgment, as, for instance, his speech on Conciliation with America, that on Economical Reform, and that to the Electors of Bristol, we find the orator to be a consummate master of the art of so constructing a speech that it serves the immediate object which prompted its delivery, while at the same time it has in it a principle of vitality which makes it survive the occasion that called it forth. But the greatest of Burke's speeches, if we look merely at the richness and variety of mental power and the force and depth of moral passion displayed in it, is his speech on the Nabob of Arcot's Debts. No speech ever delivered before any assembly, legislative, judicial, or popular, can rank with this in respect to the abundance of its facts, reasonings, and imagery, and the ferocity of its moral wrath. It resembles the El Dorado that Voltaire's Candide visited, where the boys played with precious stones of inestimable value, as our boys play with ordinary marbles; for to the inhabitants of El Dorado diamonds and pearls were as common as pebbles are with us.

But the defect of this speech, which must still be considered, on the whole, the most inspired product of Burke's great nature, was this,—that it did not strike its hearers or readers as having *reality* for its basis or the superstructure raised upon it. Englishmen could not believe then, and most of them probably do not believe now, that it had any solid foundation in incontrovertible facts. It did not "fit in" to the ordinary modes of thought; and it has never been ranked with Burke's "organized" orations; it has never come home to what Bacon called the "business and bosoms" of his countrymen. . . .

Everybody understands why any one of the great sermons of Jeremy Taylor, or the sermon of Dr. South on "Man Created in the Image of God," or the sermon of Dr. Barrow on "Heavenly Rest," differs from the millions on millions of doubtless edifying sermons that have been preached and printed during the last two centuries and a half; but everybody does not understand the distinction between one brilliant oration and another, when both made a great sensation at the time, while only one survived in literature. Probably Charles James Fox was a more effective speaker in the House of Commons than Edmund Burke; probably Henry Clay was a more effective speaker in Congress than Daniel Webster; but when the occasions on which their speeches were made are found gradually to fade from the memory of men, why is it that the speeches of Fox and Clay have no recognized position in literature, while those of Burke and Webster are ranked with literary productions of the first class? The reason is as really obvious as that which explains the exceptional value of some of the efforts of the great orators of the pulpit. Jeremy Taylor, Dr. South, and Dr. Barrow, different as they were in temper and disposition, succeeded in "organizing" some masterpieces in their special department of intellectual and moral activity; and the same is true of Burke and Webster in the departments of legislation and political science. The "occasion" was merely an opportunity for the consolidation into a speech of the rare powers and attainments, the large personality and affluent thought, which were the spiritual possessions of the man who made it,—a speech which represented the whole intellectual manhood of the speaker—a manhood in which knowledge, reason, imagination, and sensibility were all consolidated under the directing power of will.

This conception of "organization" clearly goes beyond simple structure of the parts in a speech. It deals with the impact of the orator's total resources—intellectual, emotional, and spiritual—upon a subject and an occasion. It is not, however, wholly alien to the view held by distinguished contemporary speakers. Referring to the conventional view of rhetorical order, George W. Ball tells of the "constant quarrel"—friendly, of course—with Adlai E. Stevenson over his refusal "to give his speeches a clear structure." "You are a fine poet," Ball would tell him, "but a lousy architect." Stevenson preferred to remain the poet, disdaining schematic and "pretentious pronouncements of obvious points as though 'a list were a concept or a litany a program.' "

Whether accompanied by extensive critical comment or not, this compilation like all others results from comparative inquiries. The addresses deemed worthy of inclusion and remembrance were selected because they seemed better or more representative than the scores of others with which they were matched. For permitting me to include them in this thirty-first edition, I express warm gratitude to the contributors. And to the faithful colleagues and friends whose counsel and suggestions I often solicit, I extend the usual but none the less sincere note of appreciation. Chief among them are John Jamieson and Ethel A. Crockford of The H. W. Wilson Company, Dean Keats R. McKinney of the Metropolitan State College of Colorado, Mary Margaret Robb of the University of Colorado, Dorothea Thonssen, Sandi Schloffman, Ruth Taylor, Marva McKinney, Dr. Ward Darley and Dr. E. Stewart Taylor of the University of Colorado Medical School at Denver, I. E. Levine, Director of Public Relations at the City College of New York, and Billups P. Percy of Tulane University.

LESTER THONSSEN

Denver, Colorado
September 1968

CONTENTS

IN MEMORY OF GREATNESS

OF EARTH AND SKY

THE PERSISTING AGONY

SPEECH BEFORE THE NATIONAL
LEGISLATIVE CONFERENCE [1]

LYNDON B. JOHNSON [2]

On May 3, 1968, a preliminary step was taken toward ending the fourth bloodiest war in American history. Hanoi and Washington agreed to open talks in Paris. Hopefully, this would initiate negotiations, doubtless protracted, leading to the end of a costly conflict which at best seemed to be in a state of irresolution. The war has been perilously disruptive of American loyalties, and divisively threatening to the integrity and order of the state. Be one's convictions what they may, one cannot escape the agonizing conclusion that this unpopular struggle in a remote part of the world has produced a public malaise of menacing proportions; and has blurred the image of American greatness both at home and abroad. Perhaps Americans have, in the words of President James A. McCain of Kansas State University, "like Narcissus of the Greek legend . . . suddenly discovered their image. But unlike Narcissus, they are distressed by what they see."

President Johnson has found it hard to shape his settled convictions and feelings about the war into a viable rhetoric acceptable to large segments of the population. Perhaps the war as waged since 1965 particularly is, as Max Frankel of the New York *Times* has said, "beyond all easy explanation and understanding, even if the explainer looked like Richard Burton and spoke the words of Abe Lincoln." Frankel labeled the President's difficulty as the "failure to persuade much of the country of his own deep belief that his war policy is right." Whatever the explanation, the President's efforts to mobilize massive sympathy and support for his views have not been impressively successful.

Among his many statements of the past year, two nationally televised speeches seem to epitomize his private and public attitude: the one before the National Legislative Conference at San

---

[1] Remarks of the President at San Antonio, Texas, September 29, 1967. Text furnished by the office of the Press Secretary to the President.
[2] For biographical note, see Appendix.

Antonio, Texas, on September 29, 1967; the other from the White House on March 31, 1968.

In the San Antonio address, the President did not voice a new set of beliefs or commitments. Rather, he reaffirmed vigorously his intention to continue the Vietnam war policy which the two previous Administrations had in a sense bequeathed him and which he—although he did not so declare—had obviously enlarged. Moreover, he repeated the Administration's willingness to enter upon negotiations immediately with the Hanoi government. "I am ready," he said, "to send a trusted representative of America to any spot on this earth to talk in public or private with a spokesman of Hanoi."

The importance of this address, therefore, derives not from its declaration of new principles, but from its being regarded as a sort of codified summary, or position paper. Often referred to as the San Antonio doctrine, it apparently provided ready answers to the question, "What have we done and what are we ready to do now to set the machinery of peace in motion?" "We cannot agree with all his reasoning," commented the Minneapolis *Tribune* editorially, "but we think the statement on Vietnam was needed and that the President presented his position clearly, with appropriate firmness rather than passion."

I deeply appreciate this opportunity to appear before an organization whose members contribute every day such important work to the public affairs of our state and of our country.

This evening I came here to speak to you about Vietnam.

I do not have to tell you that our people are profoundly concerned about that struggle.

There are passionate convictions about the wisest course for our nation to follow. There are many sincere and patriotic Americans who harbor doubts about sustaining the commitment that three Presidents and a half a million of our young men have made.

Doubt and debate are enlarged because the problems of Vietnam are quite complex. They are a mixture of political turmoil—of poverty—of religious and factional strife—of ancient servitude and modern longing for freedom. Vietnam is all of these things.

Vietnam is also the scene of a powerful aggression that is spurred by an appetite for conquest.

It is the arena where Communist expansionism is most aggressively at work in the world today—where it is crossing international frontiers in violation of international agreements; where it is killing and kidnapping; where it is ruthlessly attempting to bend free people to its will.

Into this mixture of subversion and war, of terror and hope, America has entered—with its material power and with its moral commitment.

Why?

Why should three Presidents and the elected representatives of our people have chosen to defend this Asian nation more than ten thousand miles from American shores?

We cherish freedom—yes. We cherish self-determination for all people—yes. We abhor the political murder of any state by another, and the bodily murder of any people by gangsters of whatever ideology. And for twenty-seven years —since the days of Lend-Lease—we have sought to strengthen free people against domination by aggressive foreign powers.

But the key to all we have done is really our own security. At times of crisis—before asking Americans to fight and die to resist aggression in a foreign land—every American President has finally had to answer this question:

Is the aggression a threat—not only to the immediate victim—but to the United States of America and to the peace and security of the entire world of which we in America are a very vital part?

That is the question which Dwight Eisenhower and John Kennedy and Lyndon Johnson had to answer in facing the issue in Vietnam.

That is the question that the Senate of the United States answered by a vote of 82 to 1 when it ratified and approved the SEATO treaty in 1955, and to which the members of the United States Congress responded in a resolution that it passed in 1964 by a vote of 504 to 2, "The United States is, therefore, prepared, as the President determines, to take all necessary steps, including the use of armed forces, to assist any member or protocol state of the Southeast Asia collective defense treaty requesting assistance in defense of its freedom."

Those who tell us now that we should abandon our commitment—that securing South Vietnam from armed domination is not worth the price we are paying—must also answer this question. And the test they must meet is this: What would be the consequence of letting armed aggression against South Vietnam succeed? What would follow in the time ahead? What kind of world are they prepared to live in five months or five years from tonight?

For those who have borne the responsibility for decision during these past ten years, the stakes to us have seemed clear —and have seemed high.

President Dwight Eisenhower said in 1959: "Strategically, South Vietnam's capture by the Communists would bring their power several hundred miles into a hitherto free region. The remaining countries in Southeast Asia would be menaced by a great flanking movement. The freedom of 12 million people would be lost immediately, and that of 150 million in adjacent lands would be seriously endangered. The loss of South Vietnam would set in motion a crumbling process that could, as it progressed, have grave consequences for us and for freedom. . . ."

And President John F. Kennedy said in 1962: ". . . Withdrawal in the case of Vietnam and the case of Thailand might mean a collapse of the entire area."

A year later, he reaffirmed that: "We are not going to withdraw from that effort. In my opinion, for us to withdraw from that effort would mean a collapse not only of South Vietnam, but Southeast Asia. So we are going to stay there."

This is not simply an American viewpoint, I would have you legislative leaders know. I am going to call the roll now of those who live in that part of the world—in the great arc of Asian and Pacific nations—and who bear the responsibility for leading their people, and the responsibility for the fate of their people.

The President of the Philippines has this to say: "Vietnam is the focus of attention now. . . . It may happen to Thailand or the Philippines, or anywhere, wherever there is misery, disease, ignorance. . . . For you to renounce your position of leadership in Asia is to allow the Red Chinese to gobble up all of Asia."

The Foreign Minister of Thailand said "[The American] decision will go down in history as the move that prevented the world from having to face another major conflagration."

The Prime Minister of Australia said: "We are there because while Communist aggression persists the whole of Southeast Asia is threatened."

President Park of Korea said: "For the first time in our history, we decided to dispatch our combat troops overseas . . . because in our belief any aggression against the Republic of Vietnam represented a direct and grave menace against the security and peace of free Asia, and therefore directly jeopardized the very security and freedom of our own people."

The Prime Minister of Malaysia warned his people that if the United States pulled out of South Vietnam, it would go to the Communists, and after that, it would only be a matter of time until they moved against neighboring states.

The Prime Minister of New Zealand said: "We can thank God that America at least regards aggression in Asia with the same concern as it regards aggression in Europe—and is prepared to back up its concern with action."

The Prime Minister of Singapore said: "I feel the fate of Asia—South and Southeast Asia—will be decided in the next few years by what happens out in Vietnam."

I cannot tell you tonight as your President—with certainty —that a Communist conquest of South Vietnam would be followed by a Communist conquest of Southeast Asia. But I do know there are North Vietnamese troops in Laos. I do know that there are North Vietnamese trained guerrillas to-night in Northeast Thailand. I do know that there are Communist-supported guerrilla forces operating in Burma. And a Communist coup was barely averted in Indonesia, the fifth largest nation in the world.

So your American President cannot tell you—with certainty—that a Southeast Asia dominated by Communist power would bring a third world war much closer to terrible reality. One could hope that this would not be so.

But all that we have learned in this tragic century strongly suggests to me that it would be so. As President of the United States, I am not prepared to gamble on the chance that it is not so. I am not prepared to risk the security—indeed, the survival—of this American nation on mere hope and wishful thinking. I am convinced that by seeing this struggle through now, we are greatly reducing the chances of a much larger war—perhaps a nuclear war. I would rather stand in Vietnam, in our time, and by meeting this danger now, and facing up to it, thereby reduce the danger for our children and for our grandchildren.

I want to turn now to the struggle in Vietnam itself.

There are questions about this difficult war that must trouble every really thoughtful person. I am going to put some of these questions. I am going to give you the very best answers that I can give you.

First, are the Vietnamese—with our help, and that of their other allies—really making any progress? Is there a forward movement? The reports I see make it clear that there is. Certainly there is a positive movement toward constitutional government. Thus far the Vietnamese have met the political schedule that they laid down in January 1966.

The people wanted an elected, responsive government. They wanted it strongly enough to brave a vicious campaign of Communist terror and assassination to vote for it. It has been said that they killed more civilians in four weeks trying to keep them from voting before the election than our American bombers have killed in the big cities of North Vietnam in bombing military targets.

On November 1, subject to the action, of course, of the constituent assembly, an elected government will be inaugurated and an elected senate and legislature will be installed. Their responsibility is clear: To answer the desires of the South Vietnamese people for self-determination and for peace, for an attack on corruption, for economic development, and for social justice.

There is progress in the war itself, steady progress considering the war that we are fighting; rather dramatic progress considering the situation that actually prevailed when we sent our troops there in 1965; when we intervened to prevent the dismemberment of the country by the Vietcong and the North Vietnamese.

The campaigns of the last year drove the enemy from many of their major interior bases. The military victory almost within Hanoi's grasp in 1965 has now been denied them. The grip of the Vietcong on the people is being broken.

Since our commitment of major forces in July 1965 the proportion of the population living under Communist control has been reduced to well under 20 per cent. Tonight the secure proportion of the population has grown from about 45 per cent to 65 per cent—and in the contested areas, the tide continues to run with us.

But the struggle remains hard. The South Vietnamese have suffered severely, as have we—particularly in the First Corps area in the North, where the enemy has mounted his heaviest attacks, and where his lines of communication to North Vietnam are shortest. Our casualties in the war have reached about 13,500 killed in action, and about 85,000 wounded. Of those 85,000 wounded, we thank God that 79,000 of the 85,000 have been returned, or will return to duty shortly. Thanks to our great American medical science and the helicopter.

I know there are other questions on your minds, and on the minds of many sincere, troubled Americans: "Why not negotiate now?" so many ask me. The answer is that we and our South Vietnamese allies are wholly prepared to negotiate tonight.

I am ready to talk with Ho Chi Minh, and other chiefs of state concerned, tomorrow.

I am ready to have Secretary Rusk meet with their Foreign Minister tomorrow.

I am ready to send a trusted representative of America to any spot on this earth to talk in public or private with a spokesman of Hanoi.

We have twice sought to have the issue of Vietnam dealt with by the United Nations—and twice Hanoi has refused.

Our desire to negotiate peace—through the United Nations or out—has been made very, very clear to Hanoi—directly and many times through third parties.

As we have told Hanoi time and time and time again, the heart of the matter really is this: The United States is willing to stop all aerial and naval bombardment of North Vietnam when this will lead promptly to productive discussions. We, of course, assume that while discussions proceed, North Vietnam would not take advantage of the bombing cessation or limitation.

But Hanoi has not accepted any of these proposals.

So it is by Hanoi's choice—and not ours, and not the rest of the world's—that the war continues.

Why, in the face of military and political progress in the South, and the burden of our bombing in the North, do they insist and persist with the war?

From many sources the answer is the same. They still hope that the people of the United States will not see this struggle through to the very end. As one Western diplomat reported to me only this week—he had just been in Hanoi— "They believe their staying power is greater than ours and that they can't lose." A visitor from a Communist capital had this to say: "They expect the war to be long, and that the

Americans in the end will be defeated by a breakdown in morale, fatigue, and psychological factors." The Premier of North Vietnam said as far back as 1962: "Americans do not like long, inconclusive war. . . . Thus we are sure to win in the end."

Are the North Vietnamese right about us?

I think not. No. I think they are wrong. I think it is the common failing of totalitarian regimes, that they cannot really understand the nature of our democracy:

They mistake dissent for disloyalty;

They mistake restlessness for a rejection of policy;

They mistake a few committees for a country;

They misjudge individual speeches for public policy.

They are no better suited to judge the strength and per-serverance of America than the Nazi and the Stalinist prop-agandists were able to judge it. It is a tragedy that they must discover these qualities in the American people, and discover them through a bloody war.

And, soon or late, they will discover them.

In the meantime, it shall be our policy to continue to seek negotiations—confident that reason will some day prevail; that Hanoi will realize that it just can never win; that it will turn away from fighting and start building for its own people.

Since World War II, this nation has met and has mastered many challenges—challenges in Greece and Turkey, in Berlin, in Korea, in Cuba.

We met them because brave men were willing to risk their lives for their nation's security. And braver men have never lived than those who carry our colors in Vietnam at this very hour.

The price of these efforts, of course, has been heavy. But the price of not having made them at all, not having seen them through, in my judgment would have been vastly greater.

Our goal has been the same—in Europe, in Asia, in our own hemisphere. It has been—and it is now—peace.

And peace cannot be secured by wishes; peace cannot be preserved by noble words and pure intentions. Enduring peace—Franklin D. Roosevelt said—cannot be bought at the cost of other people's freedom.

The late President Kennedy put it precisely in November 1961, when he said: "We are neither war mongers nor appeasers, neither hard nor soft. We are Americans determined to defend the frontiers of freedom by an honorable peace if peace is possible but by arms if arms are used against us."

The true peace-keepers in the world tonight are not those who urge us to retire from the field in Vietnam—who tell us to try to find the quickest, cheapest exit from that tormented land, no matter what the consequences to us may be.

The true peace-keepers are those men who stand out there on the DMZ [demilitarized zone] at this very hour, taking the worst that the enemy can give. The true peace-keepers are the soldiers who are breaking the terrorist's grip around the villages of Vietnam—the civilians who are bringing medical care and food and education to people who have already suffered a generation of war.

And so I report to you that we are going to continue to press forward. Two things we must do. Two things we shall do.

First, we must not mislead our enemy. Let him not think that debate and dissent will produce wavering and withdrawal. For I can assure you they won't. Let him not think that protests will produce surrender. Because they won't. Let him not think that he will wait us out. For he won't.

Second, we will provide all that our brave men require to do the job that must be done. And that job is going to be done.

These gallant men have our prayers—have our thanks—have our heart-felt praise—and our deepest gratitude.

Let the world know that the keepers of peace will endure through every trial—that with the full backing of their countrymen, they are going to prevail.

THE UNITED STATES AND VIETNAM—
WHAT LIES AHEAD [3]

MORRIS K. UDALL [4]

Few would deny that Morris K. Udall, United States Representative from the Second District of Arizona, expressed a common conviction when he called Vietnam "the overriding issue of this troubled year." Written and spoken comment for and against our involvement has been of staggering proportions. Much of it is repetitious, which is understandable and doubtless necessary since no public cause is likely to be promoted or renounced through a single or even an occasional declaration.

Morris K. Udall's speech of October 22, 1967, before the Sunday Evening Forum in Tucson, Arizona, contains two features of special interest to students of public address.

It is initially an example of what might be called the rhetoric of renunciation. A young, liberal Democrat who originally supported President Johnson's Vietnam policy, Mr. Udall did an about-face in this address and openly declared that "I was wrong two years ago, and I firmly believe President Johnson's advisers are wrong today" in the pursuit of the war aims in Southeast Asia. Admitting the difficulty and unpleasantness of giving such a speech, he declared, however, "that I would be serving neither the President nor the country to pretend to agree when I feel we must modify our national course." Following a detailed analysis of the nature and extent of our involvement, he turned to the fundamental question, How important is Vietnam in the scheme of things? "I no longer see the war in Vietnam as Munich or Valley Forge"; and, accordingly, "I propose that the United States halt all further escalation and Americanization of this war and that it discontinue sending any more Americans to do a job that ought to be done and can only be done by Vietnamese."

Like similar speeches announcing a change of opinion, this one cautiously steers a course that will at once underscore the basic differences between the old and the new conviction, and yet not give offense to the persons whose programs prompted the

[3] Sunday Evening Forum, Tucson, Arizona, October 22, 1967. Text furnished by Representative Udall, with permission for this reprint.

[4] For biographical note, see Appendix.

political apostasy. Mr. Udall's testament of dissent is forthright, fearless, and compelling.

A second feature of his address deserves notice. He relied heavily upon constructed dialogue—in this case, speech within the speech—for the development of his proposal to deescalate the war. Examine, for instance, the speeches he would invite the President to deliver by television to the American people, the people of South Vietnam, the leaders of North Vietnam, the Soviets, the Chinese, and our allies throughout the world. Similarly, Mr. Udall worded the fictional addresses which the President might direct to Ho Chi Minh, the leaders in Hanoi, and to Secretary U Thant of the United Nations.

This device has the sanction of antiquity. The ancient historiographers introduced many speeches into their narratives. Ostensibly, the talks were faithful to the original utterances of the characters; actually, they were fictional in many respects.

Perhaps the most celebrated example of constructed address in American oratorical history is Daniel Webster's supposed speech of John Adams in support of the Declaration of Independence before the Continental Congress in 1776. The speech by Adams, as well as another by an anonymous member opposing the Declaration are the best-remembered parts of Webster's "Adams and Jefferson" address at Faneuil Hall on August 2, 1826. While doubtless faithful to the ideas of Adams, the speech is nonetheless a pure construction, as Webster himself testified in a letter in 1846: "The speech was written by me, in my house, in Boston, the day before the delivery of the Discourse in Faneuil Hall; a poor substitute, I am sure it would appear to be, if we could now see the speech actually made by Mr. Adams on that transcendently important occasion."

There is a manifest difference between Daniel Webster's constructed speeches and Mr. Udall's: what Adams is represented as saying is plausibly faithful to what he might have said; what President Johnson is advised to say is an improbable version of what he would not consider saying in the first place. But the rhetorical techniques are comparable.

Tonight I come to talk about war and peace, about Presidents, dominoes, commitments and mistakes. I want to start with some of my own commitments and at least one of my own mistakes.

When I went to Congress six years ago I made some commitments to myself: to make the tough and unpleasant decisions as they came; to speak out at times when remaining silent might be easier; to admit my own mistakes; and to advocate new policies when old ones, no matter how dearly held, had failed.

Two years ago, when this country had fewer than 50,000 men in Vietnam, I wrote a newsletter defending the President's Vietnam policy and pleading patience and understanding for what he was trying to do. I have thought about that newsletter many times with increasing dismay and doubt as the limited involvement I supported has grown into a very large Asian land war with half a million American troops scattered in jungles and hamlets, fighting an enemy who is everywhere and nowhere, seeking to save a country which apparently doesn't want to be saved, with casualties mounting and no end in sight, with more and more troops being asked for and sent, and with the dangers of World War III looming ever larger.

In the past two or three years I have attended many Vietnam briefings of the White House and State Department. Every time I've been told things are starting to look up. The "crossover point" may be just around the corner. The "kill rate" is usually up. The pacification program, despite difficulties, is showing "real progress." Enemy morale is always down; in fact, each report brings new evidence of gloom for the enemy's forces. And the South Vietnamese army is always beginning to be ready to fight instead of run.

To be fair about it, I presume some progress has resulted from our enormous expenditures in lives and resources. I would hate to think otherwise. But each American escalation has been matched by escalation on the other side. And the grim probability as I speak tonight is that new and bigger escalations lie ahead. Unless we change our policy I predict we will have 750,000 troops committed to Vietnam within the next eighteen months. There will be more bombing, more civilian deaths in South and North Vietnam, more American casualties, and great new demands on the American taxpayers to pay for all this.

I have listened to all the arguments of the Administration, read all the reports available to me, attended all the briefings, heard all the predictions of an eventual end to hostilities, and I still conclude that we're on a mistaken and dangerous road. In my judgment continuing our present policy will require that we send several hundred thousand more American troops to thresh around almost aimlessly in the jungles of Vietnam, thousands more of them dying and many more losing arms and legs and eyes without ever achieving what we know as "victory," all the while the material cost of this war is climbing from the present thirty billion dollars a year to forty or fifty or more.

What's even worse, I increasingly fear that the inevitable result of this policy will be a wider war. Already the major battles along the Demilitarized Zone are bringing talk of an invasion of the North, and as our bombers get ever closer to the Chinese border and Russian ships in Haiphong, one can see the stakes in this contest rising. I know there are those who say Russia and China would be foolish to come in with all the advantages they are enjoying from the present stalemate. But these people and this line of thinking were wrong in Korea, and they may well be wrong again.

Many of the wise old heads in Congress say privately that the best politics in this situation is to remain silent, to fuzz your views on this great issue, and to await developments. I hear few dovish noises in Arizona, and I suspect that silence would be the best personal politics for me. This would be especially true if it should turn out that we are at last starting to "win" this war.

Then why am I here tonight? Vietnam is the overriding issue of this troubled year, and the people of my state are as entitled to my honest views as I am to theirs. I have come here tonight to say as plainly and simply as I can that I was wrong two years ago, and I firmly believe President Johnson's advisers are wrong today. Victory may indeed lie ahead; nothing is certain in this life. But life goes on, and men must make decisions based on the best information available to them at the time. Waiting for things to happen is not leadership, and steering a safe political course is not the highest order of public service.

This speech is not an easy or pleasant task for me. I am of the President's party; I admire him and the great things he has done for America. I have defended him on a great many occasions, including a visit I made to Cambridge University in England last February when my questioners were highly critical of our role in Vietnam. I know from history and from observing two Presidents firsthand what a man-killing job the presidency is. So I take no satisfaction in disagreeing with a policy he feels he must pursue. I respect President Johnson for doing what he firmly believes is right, and it grieves me to add to his burdens. But I would be serving neither the President nor the country to pretend to agree when I feel we must modify our national course.

As I look back over the last two years I see the United States mounting a treadmill that goes ever faster—so fast it seems almost impossible now to get off. Yet I am convinced that we must get off that treadmill and that we can. The hour is late, but I believe this nation of ours has the brains, the know-how, the courage, the imagination to begin to extricate itself from a war we should never have blundered into.

Now, I don't want to fool you or myself. The steps I will propose in a moment will cost something, too, and, if taken, may have convulsive effects for a time in our own national life. But, in my judgment, the costs of staying with a mistaken policy will be far greater.

The great rationalization for our involvement in Vietnam is that we are there to stop the march of communism, to demonstrate that the United States honors its commitments, to strengthen the free world. We are failing, and I believe we will continue to fail as long as we maintain our present policy of military escalation. Indeed, I believe this policy is strengthening the Communist cause, weakening the free world, and raising grave doubts about the capacity of the United States to back up its commitments elsewhere.

I am advocating a change, not out of any fear or love for communism or admiration of Ho Chi Minh, but out of love for America and for its national aspirations. I am convinced our present policy in Vietnam does not serve our interests, and in a way it is as though we had designed it to serve our enemies. This may seem too utterly ironic, but let's think about it for a minute.

Let's suppose there had been a world Communist meeting in, say, July 1964. Everything was in disarray. The once-monolithic Communist movement was in a shambles. The two major Red powers, the Soviet Union and China, were at each other's throats. The Russians had suffered humiliating reverses in Berlin, Cuba, Africa and elsewhere. I recall *U.S. News & World Report* the previous fall had published an article entitled, "Is Russia Losing the Cold War?," and concluded that it was.

Suppose that at this imaginary meeting a brilliant young theorist had come forward with a dramatic plan to reverse the unhappy trend. Let me recite what he might have said.

"Comrades, I have a plan. By means of it we can enmesh the United States in the Asian land war its leaders have always warned against. Within three years I promise you 500,000 American soldiers will be hopelessly bogged down in jungle fighting, consuming huge amounts of supplies and vast quantities of ammunition while gaining essentially nothing. They will be seen as white men fighting Asiatics, colonialists, burning villages, destroying rice crops, killing and maiming women and children. Their casualties will be heavy—perhaps 100,000 by late 1967. They will have to boost their draft quotas and raise taxes. The war will cost them $30 billion or more a year. And this will upset their economy, cause inflation, threaten their balance of payments, and play hob with all their domestic programs. There will be great internal dissension and even riots in their cities. And, comrades, in spite of our differences, this is one cause that will bring us together, fighting on the same side. Furthermore, we can achieve all these wonderful results without committing a single Russian or Chinese soldier, sailor or airman, and at a total cost of perhaps one or two billion a year."

This is sheer invention, of course. There was no such meeting and no such plan. But the fact is that a dedicated President, surrounded by advisers with the highest patriotism and aided by a well-meaning but pliant Congress—all with the best of intentions—has achieved essentially these results. We have handed our enemies all of this on a platter, and today many sincere Americans are ready to hand them a lot more of the same.

What we are doing today, as I see it, is essentially engaging in an act of national rationalization. We talk about having no alternatives, but if you boil that down to its essence, what it means is that we're too big and powerful to admit we made a mistake. I refuse any longer to accept a tortured logic which allows little mistakes to be admitted, but requires *big* ones to be pursued to the bitter end, regardless of their cost in lives and money. As a nation let's not adopt the senseless psychology of the compulsive gambler at the race track. If he's lost a whole week's wages on some unfortunate nag, he ought to quit and go home, sadder but wiser. But no, he'll go to the bank, draw out his savings, mortgage his house, and wipe out his children's chances for a college education, all in the vain hope that he can recoup his losses. I think this is the direction we're headed in Vietnam.

When I talk to people about this war, I find them most troubled by this fundamental question:

Why is it that the United States, the most powerful, efficient and successful nation on earth, can't defeat a little, miserable, backward country like North Vietnam and do it overnight—or at least in six days like the Israelis?

On the face of it it *is* ridiculous. But there is logic and reason behind every event if we will only search for it. There are answers to this tough question—and they make sense—if we'll only look the truth in the face. Those answers as I see them come down to four fundamental propositions:

You cannot win a political and guerrilla war in South Vietnam by any amount of bombing in North Vietnam. President Johnson knows this, but I don't think the people do. Too many, I suspect, think that more bombs can win the war.

You cannot win this kind of war when the government you are backing is largely run by wealthy landowners and a military elite who have no real interest in the poor, illiterate peasants over whom the war is being fought. Unless they will give their support to that government, any military victory will be short-lived, if it can be achieved at all.

You cannot save a people who do not want to be saved and will not fight for the government which runs their lives.

You cannot win in this deadly poker game when any escalation "bet" on your part can be matched by a much smaller escalation on the part of the enemy. We cannot continue to assume that when we increase our forces the other side will stand still giving us a clear margin of superiority. Every time the result has been the same: stalemate, at an even higher and more dangerous and costly level.

These are the grim truths about Vietnam, as I see them; before I go on I want to discuss them just a little further.

Our policy seems to assume you can win this kind of war in South Vietnam with a bombing sideshow in North Vietnam. In my judgment there simply isn't a cheap, easy, sanitary way you can convert the people of South Vietnam into supporting the kind of government we've seen in Saigon, and that is what the war is all about.

It should be starkly clear to everyone by now that our bombing policy has failed. It began with *two* objectives—to stop or restrict the flow of men and materials to the south, *and* to bring Hanoi to the conference table. It has done neither.

In January 1965, the enemy strength over-all was about 120,000. Today, despite huge casualties, it's estimated at

296,000. If we could believe all these Pentagon body counts, the North Vietnamese and Vietcong lost 149,000 men in 1966 alone. And yet their forces have doubled in size. By the math of guerrilla warfare which requires that we outnumber them at least 4 to 1, the Communists have more than matched our build-up to 500,000 men.

As far as the other objective is concerned, President Johnson tells us he hasn't heard from Hanoi. So apparently the bombing hasn't accomplished anything on that score either. Indeed, the strange fact is that stopping the bombing might bring talks; continuing it almost surely won't.

You know, when I hear people say we aren't bombing enough—and that is their explanation for our failures—I wonder what kind of scale they're using. I presume most of you were living during World War II, and you recall the merciless, intense bombing raids the Germans made upon England and the far greater devastation we rained upon the major cities of Europe in 1944-45. The peak was about 80,000 tons of bombs a month, yet we're dropping more than that now on a little country half the size of Arizona.

The fact is, we've substantially destroyed the production facilities of North Vietnam. Since their war materials are now coming from factories in China and Russia which we aren't able to bomb, it is argued that we must destroy the goods in transit, no matter what risks are involved.

I wonder how many people really believe the issues in Vietnam are worth the risk of a larger war. Vietnam is a nation whose history has been marked by turmoil, and by sporadic warring between North and South, for a thousand years. It is a nation that has known oppression at the hands of the Chinese, Japanese and French. It has never been able to develop a strong national government. The only government the people ever see is the tax collector. Some of the areas we are trying to liberate today haven't paid allegiance to Saigon for years. In fact, the whole history of Vietnam is one of local autonomy and great hostility to any central government, and one of the reasons so many local officials have been murdered by the Vietcong is that they were imposed on the villages by the Saigon government. This is where the struggle lies. We are fighting to preserve the residue of French colonialism in Indochina—an oligarchy of well-to-do, landed beneficiaries of a century of French rule. And when I read that absentee landlords often follow our troops into former Vietcong areas—to collect back rent as high as 60 per cent of the total rice production—I wonder how much chance we have of ever winning this struggle.

I sincerely hope that the recent election represents a turn toward popular government and attention to the needs of the people. And I recognize the problem of trying to build a nation in the midst of a civil war. But thus far there has been little to give one a feeling of encouragement.

I wonder if you realize just how discouraging the situation is. Officer commissions in South Vietnam can be bought. Military supplies are stolen constantly. For many, bribery is a way of life. And in three years of fighting, out of 600,000 South Vietnamese, I understand only one officer of the rank of major or above has been wounded, and none has been killed. Can ordinary men be expected to follow leaders like this?

I might mention that through February of this year the United States lost, not one or two, but 109 of its officers of the rank of major or above in this military action. The number is even higher today.

As an American I also feel considerable resentment that our young men are required to risk their lives in Vietnam while that nation permits perhaps 200,000 of its own young men to dodge the draft and another 100,000 or more to desert the army every year. And it is shocking to me to realize that young Vietnamese can be deferred from the draft to go to college even if they never show up in class.

I suppose the average American imagines that our soldiers over there are spending their time fighting North Vietnamese who have infiltrated to the South. Let's not fool ourselves about who is fighting whom. Eighty per cent of the troops opposing us are South Vietnamese. Recently along the De-militarized Zone we have been fighting some North Viet-namese main force units, but these constitute only a small portion of what we call "the enemy." The truth is that in most battles *Americans* are fighting *South Vietnamese*. I ask you: what are we doing? What are Arizona boys doing fighting South Vietnamese on behalf of other South Vietnamese whose leaders lack the will to fight?

I said earlier that we are fighting this war on the enemy's terms and with the odds stacked against us. Let me give you an example.

An American lieutenant recently talked to a news corre-spondent as he viewed the battle in a valley. Three heli-copters were fluttering over a jungle area and shots were ringing out. The officer observed, "Look at this. I have $3 million worth of equipment and twelve or fifteen highly-trained, well-educated men. Opposed to them over in that clearing is one peasant with a $50 gun. If the peasant is lucky, he wins the whole ball game."

Or think about this. We may gamble a $2 million air-plane, $10,000 worth of bombs and the priceless life of an American pilot against a $25 rope bridge which will be re-built tomorrow even if we're lucky to make a direct hit. These are the odds we're playing over there.

Where does all this end? Already it has cost us close to $100 billion and over 100,000 casualties. And what have we gained for our country, for Vietnam, or for the cause of free-dom? The time has come, I believe, to look at this war to see what we stand to gain by continuing our present policy —or to lose by trying some other policy.

The fundamental question is: How important is Vietnam in the scheme of things? Is this Armageddon? Is this the ultimate test of strength between government by consent and government by coercion, between capitalism and commu-nism? Is the government of South Vietnam the one whose existence will determine the future course of civilization? Is this the showdown for the concept of "wars of national liberation?" Will this really determine whether our grand-children live under communism? Does it really mean that we'll only have to fight later in Hawaii, Oregon or Arizona? If the answers to these questions are "yes," then we must proceed at all cost to win this war and insulate the government of South Vietnam from all future attack, subversion or rebellion.

But suppose, as I believe, that this is not Armageddon. Suppose this is just one of many episodes of revolution and turmoil occurring, and about to occur, in a world that is seething with the forces of change. Suppose that our extremely costly and exhausting response to this episode reveals to our enemies that we obviously can't afford to go through this process again soon. Suppose that a very possible result of this fantastically expensive enterprise will be a delay of just a few years in the ultimate success of the National Liberation Front. If this is the case, then I believe we must put greater emphasis upon our goals as a nation and less on the immediate military goals proposed for the conduct of this war.

I have reflected long and hard on what this war is, what significance it holds, and what effects various courses of action would have on our future role in world affairs. And I will tell you frankly I no longer see the war in Vietnam as Munich or Valley Forge. And I'm no longer very interested in hearing how we can capture one more hamlet or rocky hill. I'm interested in hearing how we can cut our losses, reduce our future expenditures in lives and resources, and bring this venture down to scale. I'm convinced our national interest—not Russia's, not China's, not North Vietnam's—demands that we sharply modify our present policy and that we start doing so now.

A great fallacy of our present policy, as I see it, lies in the assumption that stopping this "war of national liberation" will prevent any and all future wars of this type. Such wars were beaten back in Malaysia and Korea, yet this did not stop Vietnam or Cuba or the Congo. We are only due for more frustration and anger in the years ahead if we spend more blood and treasure to get some kind of significant "victory" in Vietnam.

This brings me to the hard question the President's advisers always put to their critics: "All right, you don't like what we're doing. Precisely what would you do, and what are the likely results of your policy?"

This is a fair question that demands an answer. I'll tell you what I propose, but first let me make clear what I do *not* propose.

We are in South Vietnam. It was a mistake to get there, but we're there. I am not suggesting any "cut and run" policy or proposing that the United States now withdraw from this war at once. I am not suggesting that we surrender to Ho Chi Minh. I am not suggesting that we turn our backs on those in South Vietnam who have come to rely on our commitments—people who, if we departed, might be victims in a blood bath of the kind we saw in Indonesia. I am not suggesting that this country violate the limited commitments we originally made. I do not propose that our investment in American blood and money be abandoned without giving the South Vietnamese every reasonable chance to save themselves.

And let me make clear there is another thing I am not doing. I am not breaking with President Johnson, either as Chief Executive or as leader of my party. Nor am I joining that group of anarchists who are marching on Washington, attempting to block the entrances of the Pentagon, counseling defiance of Selective Service, or sending money to the Vietcong.

Furthermore, I am not proposing anything particularly new. I don't pretend to have all the classified information necessary to formulate detailed alternatives. Rather, like Senators Mansfield, Church, Cooper, Morton, Percy and others who appreciate the President's sincerity and his anguish over the progress of this war, I feel I must try to convince him that our present policy is wrong and should be changed or modified.

Now, what *do* I propose? I propose that the United States halt all further escalation and Americanization of this war and that it discontinue sending any more Americans to do a job that ought to be done and can only be done by Vietnamese. I am suggesting that we deescalate and de-Americanize this war and that we begin the slow, deliberate and painful job of extricating ourselves from a hopeless, openended "commitment" we never made. I am suggesting that we start bringing American boys home and start turning this war back to the Vietnamese. I am suggesting that we offer the people of Southeast Asia something better than the prospect of Vietnam-type wars as an answer to threats of subversion or aggression.

I would say to President Johnson: facing this decision will take the courage and greatness of which you are capable. People will vilify you, or accuse you of appeasement. Countless armchair generals will tell you victory was just around the corner. But in the end I believe the American people will rally behind you when they realize that this decision will strengthen our country and advance its interests.

Major policy changes are tough to explain and defend, but I would propose that the President go on television and speak plainly to the American people, to the people of South Vietnam, to the leaders of North Vietnam, to the Soviets and the Chinese, and to our allies and friends around the world. I would propose that he tell them something like this:

"I didn't start this war but I enlarged it. I did this in the honest belief it could be won at moderate cost. My best advice in 1964 was that fewer than 100,000 troops would do the job. This didn't work. I was told that 300,000 would do the job. This didn't work either. Then I was told 500,000 was enough. It isn't. Now I'm hearing that another 100,000 or 200,000 will be the magic number. I was told that bombing extensively in the North would stop infiltration and bring Hanoi to the peace table. Instead, infiltration has increased as we have increased the bombing, and we're farther from the peace table than when we began. On the basis of all this advice we're dropping more bombs on this small, miserable country than the allies dropped on Europe at the peak of World War II, and yet our objectives elude us. So far I've seen 700 of our most costly aircraft destroyed and 1500 of our best pilots downed. I've seen 15,000 of our young men killed and 85,000 wounded, and countless others confined under unspeakable conditions in Communist prisons.

"I tell you frankly, my fellow citizens, that my advice was wrong and the decisions I made were wrong. As your President I now refuse to compound these mistakes, to follow this advice any longer, or to subject you and your sons and your tax dollars anymore to a course which is defeating this country's interests and dividing its people. I happen to believe that the pacification of Detroit and Newark is at least as important as the pacification of jungle hamlets in South Vietnam —and we can't do both.

"Accordingly, I am ordering a halt to the bombing of North Vietnam. I am ordering a gradual deescalation of our entire war effort and I am directing our military men to prepare plans to back our troops off within a reasonable time to those areas of South Vietnam which can be defended most readily and to turn over the remaining defense job to the South Vietnamese themselves. Within a reasonable time after that we will turn over the balance of this war effort to the South Vietnamese and bring virtually all our troops back home. In keeping with our commitments, we will continue to supply whatever is needed to maintain the South Vietnamese forces while this threat continues and as long as we are convinced the government of South Vietnam is working in the interest of its own people."

The President having done this, I would suggest that he call upon our allies in the free world to assist this country in formulating a program of land reform, economic development, health and education throughout Southeast Asia, and that he ask the Congress to authorize a small part of the money saved through reduction of our war effort for a fund to begin this program.

Finally, I would suggest that the President send a message to the eight nations which participated with us in the Geneva Convention of 1954. It is in the breakdown of that convention—and the United States carries a large share of responsibility for that breakdown—that one finds the seeds of the conflict in Vietnam today. I would have him propose that the nations which were a party to that convention reconvene at the earliest possible date to set up procedures for a cessation of hostilities and for a return to the principles of that convention.

Now, what about our allies—and our enemies? To the elected leaders of South Vietnam I would think the President might say something like this:

"Our commitment to you was to assist you in repelling external aggression, not in defending your central government from your own people. We promised to help you build a free and non-Communist government, not to perpetuate a military or unrepresentative regime. Insofar as we have seen this war in terms of invasion from the North we have felt obligated to honor these commitments, and we have done so at tremendous cost in lives and in dollars. Wherever we have met main force units of the North Vietnamese, we have defeated them decisively. We are not leaving just yet, but we're cutting back because we think it is time for you to do your own fighting. This is your country and your war, not ours. And if your own people need pacifying, only you can pacify them; we can't begin to do a job like that. You must now build an army which can win this war; we can't win it for you. We will provide you with supplies and ammunition, but we are tired of cheating and black-marketing and stealing while your people laugh at us. And a condition for our support will be stern measures by your government to bring these practices to an end.

"You have had your elections now, and it is up to you to begin immediately to build a government which will root out corruption and nepotism, and that will be concerned about the health and education and safety of ordinary people. If you will do this, we will help you finance a new program of public health, education, economic development and land reform that can provide a stable base for peace in Vietnam and Southeast Asia.

"I think it is time that you give more than lip service to the principles you espoused in Geneva—a unified Vietnam and free and open elections, both North and South. This war is more than a conflict between abstract ideologies, more than a chess game between the Communist and non-Communist worlds. This war is mainly a product of real forces at work in your own country. No matter how difficult these problems are, you the people of Vietnam ought to be working at them. We Americans cannot settle these differences, but perhaps you can."

To Ho Chi Minh and the other leaders in Hanoi I would suggest the President say something like this:

"We have beaten your main force units in every engagement, and we can continue to do so indefinitely. But we don't choose to do so because this is your kind of war, not ours. No longer will American troops contest you for every ridge, hill or patch of jungle. You will now be fighting your fellow countrymen. If you choose to fight our forces while they remain in Vietnam, you're going to have to attack us in strongly fortified areas where we have all the advantages. And this is going to be the new fact of life for you in Vietnam. No longer are we basing our plans on forcing you to the conference table in a hurry with one escalation after another. We're settling down now and building a firm base for the government of South Vietnam —but we're ready, too, to return to Geneva and to the principle of a unified Vietnam.

"Furthermore, if you want to continue fighting, you should understand that you can take absolutely nothing for granted. While we will confine ourselves principally to certain areas of South Vietnam, the South Vietnamese will be everywhere, and we will not hestitate to come out and spoil offensive preparations directed against those areas we control when we feel so inclined. And whatever happens, American air power and naval power will remain in the Pacific.

"You have said a halt to the bombing of North Vietnam might persuade you to negotiate. Note that I am ordering a halt to the bombing. I suggest you now have an obligation to meet your part of the bargain."

To our allies and those nations of the world which have complained of our bombing and escalation policies I think the President might say this:

"These policies you objected to have ended. Now let's see what you can do to find an avenue to peace in Vietnam."

To Secretary U Thant of the United Nations he might say:

"You talked a lot about our bombing operations blocking any hope for peace. Now here is your chance. If the Russians really want peace, as you have suggested, if an end to the bombing can bring an end to the war, let us now see results. Let *both* sides deescalate. Let the Russians now deescalate their supply operation. Let them show good faith in their state-ments about bringing this matter to the conference table—either that or stop talking peace while making war."

There you have it—a plan I believe might start to get us off the Vietnam treadmill. I frankly admit there is nothing very heroic about it. It's a far cry from "damn the torpedoes," "surrender, hell, we've just begun to fight," and other such stirring phrases from our history. But I think it is a prudent and humane proposal which will advance our country's interests. I'm just enough of an optimist to believe that a dramatic change of this kind would command support from a large majority of American mothers and fathers and sons and taxpayers and people who are concerned about the problems of our cities and our environment. I'm optimist enough to believe that a majority of our citizens regard the welfare of this country and the peace of the world as more important than "saving face," whatever that means. This country wants leadership, and it has always wanted to be told the truth—even the unpleasant truth.

I don't know how the ornithologists ever got involved in this war, and I have little hope that this speech won't get me labeled as some variety of dove, chicken hawk, pigeon, owl or ostrich. However, if it should happen that I dropped dead leaving this meeting tonight, I would hope that my tombstone might read: "Here lies a realist." Not a hawk, not a dove, but a man who was willing to face painful and unpleasant realities. It is my judgment that both the so-called "hawks" and "doves" have erred in our recent debate over Vietnam and that both have been unrealistic, in part, in what they have advocated. I will return to this in a moment, and I'll have some critical things to say to each.

In this life every choice has its consequences. It isn't enough to complain of a policy one doesn't like; one must have alternatives and be prepared to face their consequences. I realize that my proposals, too, will have some pretty distasteful ramifications. But I'm willing to face them, as I expect I will have to do in the question period tonight.

Because I think so much of our debate on Vietnam has been up in the clouds, I'd like to take a moment here to face up to five hard, stern realities which limit our options over there. Two of them the "hawks" refuse to face; three of them tend to be ignored by the "doves."

The *first* of these is that no amount of bombing is going to stop transportation of enough supplies to keep the Communist effort going in the South. The supplies aren't made in North Vietnam. They are made in Russia and China. If we permanently destroyed every railroad track and every bridge in the North, enough supplies would go through to keep this war at the present level indefinitely, and we have this on the word of Secretary McNamara in sworn testimony before the Senate. In 1966 the North Vietnamese were sending about 100 tons a day into the South. Today, following a year of the most intensive bombing in the history of the world, they're not sending 100 tons—they're sending 300 tons a day. And yet we are told that 100,000 tons of bombs a month, instead of 80,000 will change the result.

The *second* of these stern realities is directed to those who write me saying, "Let's pull out the stops." I wonder if they have thought about where this will lead. As you know, the United States got into this mess through certain commitments made by a succession of Presidents. Other nations have made commitments, too. When commitments like this come into direct conflict, wars get started. Political scientists still like to play games with the combination of treaties and ententes and obligations of various kinds existing among the nations of Europe prior to World War I.

My second reality, then, is this: No living man can give us any assurance that Russia or China, or both, won't come into this war with both feet in the next week, or month, or year, if we keep on as we are. As a realist I have to agree that the odds are they will not. But what a crazy gamble. If we lose that gamble, we are talking not of 500,000 American troops and $30 billion a year but perhaps five million troops and

$300 billion a year—and maybe nuclear warheads on Tucson and every other important city.

Let's not forget Korea. Recall that President Truman met with General MacArthur on Wake Island on October 15, 1950, and in that conference MacArthur told Truman the war was all but won and assured him neither the Russians nor Chinese would intervene in spite of our invading North Korea. With Truman's acquiescence MacArthur proceeded to launch a "final" offensive on November 25, followed one day later by Chinese intervention and one of the most costly retreats in American history. We ignored reality then; let's not repeat it.

I gather that among the "birds" here tonight are some "doves." I have some hard counsel for you, too. Many of you have written saying that if we will but stop the bombing, Ho Chi Minh will join us in sincere talks. I hope I'm wrong, but I have to tell you of my *third* stern reality—the improbability that Hanoi will pull our chestnuts out of the fire, or help us find some easy way to save face. I've studied the arguments about past peace efforts and the charges that we resumed bombing just as negotiations were about to begin. Our peace efforts have been clumsy, and probably insufficient, but I don't believe that Hanoi in the past three years has really been willing to make a peace our government would have accepted. The President was encouraged last winter to make something out of the "Tet" truce, and we stopped our bombing activities for a few days. Knowing this was coming, the North Vietnamese loaded up every truck and sampan they could find, and in those four days moved really huge amounts of supplies. But they didn't move a single diplomat, or a single peace feeler.

In spite of this gloomy peace prospect I think my program makes sense because it's right for our country. I'm tired of having decisions affecting 200 million Americans being determined by what some hard-nosed Politburo in Hanoi or Peking decides to do.

And this brings me to stern reality number *four*. There are legitimate, effective, democratic means available to work a change in the policies of our government. They still work, and I'm trying to use one of them tonight. Violence and disruption and name-calling will contribute nothing to the solution of our problems or the advancement of reasonable alternatives.

If alternatives are to be regarded as more than mere posturing, they cannot start with the assumption that anyone taking a different view is ignorant of the facts, blind to truth, oblivious to history and basically wicked. Reasonable men can differ on the course to follow in Vietnam, and they're not likely to come to agreement through the shaking of fists or flinging of epithets.

Thinking about the consequences of my proposal, I feel I must face up to one *final* very harsh reality, and that is the slim prospect that the present government of South Vietnam and its army will be able to do the job I have outlined for them. On this level I am frankly pessimistic about my proposal. But if we give them a fair chance, if we assure them of all the supplies and ammunition and military hardware they need, and in spite of this they are unable to manage their own defense after a reasonable length of time, then so be it. The Lord has not assigned us the job of defending South Vietnam in perpetuity. The French withdrew from Indochina and Algeria. Britain did the same in India, Egypt and various countries of Africa. The Dutch did it in Indonesia. There were internal convulsions in each case, but those nations survived and prospered.

How ironic it is that we can live in this prosperous country and go calmly to bed at night while governments which call themselves "Communist" rule in Warsaw or Budapest, or indeed Havana. But we must accept tens of thousands of American casualties and put out endless billions of dollars to assure, at all cost, that there is never such a government in Saigon. I'd far prefer to see friendly governments in all of

Asia; but there are limits to what this country can do and to the costs I'm willing to pay.

I have always wondered why it is that every other country can lose wars, admit mistakes and retreat once in a while, all without permanent injury, but the United States can do none of these things without loss of honor.

I say let's continue to supply South Vietnam. Let's make clear we will withdraw our forces gradually. But in the end let's put the destiny of Vietnam in the hands of the Vietnamese, and let's get back to our own serious problems in this country.

As I speak tonight we're about a year from our next presidential election. Nearly everyone, I suppose, has been speculating about the choices that will face us in that contest. If the Republicans reveal more judgment than I tend to credit them with, they might present us with an option such as I have outlined tonight. If they do that, there might well be a Republican President in the White House in 1969. But I don't think they will give us this kind of option. I expect their candidate will be a Nixon or a Reagan who promises us even more bombing and more escalation and more likelihood of blundering into World War III. And the end result, after more years of bloodshed, bombs and war bonds—if we're lucky—will be some kind of cessation of hostilities without victory. And then a few years later some Asian Charles de Gaulle will boot us out, and we will have gained nothing but bitterness and debt.

I might say that, if President Johnson could work some miracle and get a cease-fire tomorrow, I would expect this same result a few years hence. Charles de Gaulle may be a unique personage but he has no monopoly on ingratitude.

As I spoke of the consequences of my proposal, I'm sure some were saying, "Yes, but how about the Domino Theory?" My answer is that countries aren't dominoes, and wars aren't games. What's going on in Vietnam can't be explained simply in terms of a world ideological struggle. There are real issues involved in Vietnam and the other countries of Southeast

Asia. A country that ignores these real problems is headed for trouble. A country that works at solving its problems probably is going to make out all right.

If you want my best judgment regarding the Domino Theory, it is that our military operations in Laos and Thailand have made those countries far more likely to topple, like dominoes, than if we had never fought in Southeast Asia at all.

That brings me to the subject of commitments. Last spring in a House speech I quoted historian Henry Steele Commager as saying that the succession of commitments we have made in Vietnam were essentially "mindless." I agreed with this and said it was as though at each of the crucial moments when world-shaking decisions were to be made we had our minds on other matters and regarded these decisions as of little consequence. I still believe this, and as a member of Congress I regret that our Presidents in the last twenty years have committed this nation to assume certain obligations without fully consulting the Congress or initiating any dialogue that could produce a clear mandate for such commitments.

Each of these commitments was made, I believe, with the assumption that this was all that was needed to carry out United States objectives in Vietnam. Now we are told that with just another 45,000 troops, and perhaps bombing of the last remaining targets in North Vietnam, we can do the job. Who really believes this?

Some years ago, when I was practicing law here, a troubled businessman of modest means came to me as an old friend. His closest friend during a terminal illness had asked him to help the sick man's son, who was just starting in business. He readily agreed; in other words, he made a solemn commitment. Subsequently he loaned the boy $5,000 after his friend's death. It soon became apparent the boy didn't have any business sense, but the agreement was a solemn one. Soon he had $25,000 of his own money and half his working hours invested in a clearly losing venture, and he was neglecting his own business affairs. When he came to see me, he had just talked with his banker about mortgaging his home. It was apparent to me he was on a course that would lead eventually to bankruptcy.

I believe the "war hawks" in this country are following a similar sort of logic. They say it was a mistake to commit ourselves, but we did, and therefore we have no alternative but to carry it on at any cost, no matter how great or for how long, until we can conclude it on terms which we consider satisfactory.

I told my Tucson friend that he had kept the spirit and word of any commitment he had made to his dead friend and that now he should tell the boy frankly that he could go no further. I told him, as I tell my countrymen now, that your first commitment is to your own people and your own future. Beyond this you do what you reasonably can for your friends, but no more.

Finally, I'd like to talk about that magic national attribute called "face." As I recall, this is something we used to say the Orientals were terribly concerned about. Now apparently it's become vital to us.

I don't accept this. In the long run a nation's prestige and greatness and "face" depend on doing what is right for its own people and taking the consequences. There is no dignity greater than that of a strong man, or strong nation, admitting a mistake, correcting it, and taking the consequences. There is no course more likely in the long run to destroy one's dignity or "face" than to become a prisoner of past mistakes.

I'm against Communist aggression and for building up the strength of the free world, and this is why I propose that we quit playing a Communist game on Communist terms. I propose that we put greater emphasis on America's self-interest.

Perhaps this sounds isolationist. Well, I'm no isolationist. I don't think America can or should turn its back on the world. With the population explosion, technological development and all the rest, it's vital that we play a role in world affairs. But I do not believe the Lord ever put his foot on Plymouth Rock and assigned us the mission to settle every controversy in every corner of the world. In the past quarter-century we seem to have taken on such a role.

What we must do is put Vietnam in perspective. If we could but read the history of the coming century, I think we would see that the struggle in Vietnam was but one of dozens of struggles in the underdeveloped, formerly colonial areas of Asia and Africa and Latin America. There are great forces of change at work in the world, and I'm not talking about communism. I'm talking about the aspirations of two thirds of the human race to enjoy the good life now enjoyed by the other third. We can't prevent change from occurring, even if we wanted to do so. And we can't police the world and right every wrong.

By policing Vietnam we hope to make our commitments credible, yet increasingly we are making them less credible. To illustrate, earlier this year the President dispatched three lonely transports to the Congo to aid in quelling the latest eruption there. It provoked a violent storm of congressional criticism on the grounds that it represented the first step toward another Vietnam involvement. I'm not saying the criticism was right or wrong, but this episode reveals the hard truth that, precisely because of Vietnam, the United States is far less likely ever again to intervene in places where intervention is favorable, is called for, or might be successful.

There are some 125 nations in this world. In the years ahead many of them are going to be involved in civil wars, revolutions and clashes with their neighbors. In most cases our best policy will be to stand back, as we did in Indonesia, the fifth largest nation in the world, a rich source of many raw materials, an area far more important in any power struggle than Vietnam. For years this nation had what amounted to a Communist government under Sukarno. He broke relations with the United States, burned our libraries, denounced us at every turn. Surely here was a situation touching our interests. Yet we committed not a single soldier nor for many months a single dollar of aid. What was the result? Because we stood back and waited, the people of that country took matters into their own hands and threw Sukarno and his Communist friends out. While many problems still beset it, Indonesia has started on a better course.

In Vietnam the task has been made infinitely more difficult by our actions of the past two decades, but we can still help the Vietnamese people to do the same thing for themselves. And, in any case, we should know by now that we can't do it for them.

The world has always been full of evil, suffering and injustice. I wish it were not so. But I agree with President Kennedy who said not so many years ago:

We must face the fact that the United States is neither omnipotent or omniscient—that we are only 6 per cent of the world's population—that we cannot impose our will on the other 94 per cent of mankind—that we cannot right every wrong or reverse each adversity—and therefore there cannot be an American solution to every world problem.

I agree with these words of President Kennedy, yet I am also aware that he shares with Presidents Truman, Eisenhower and Johnson a partial responsibility for the fix we are in today in Vietnam. To me, this contradiction illustrates the dilemma of America's postwar role as a world leader. We have no territorial designs. We believe in the free determination of people to choose their own form of government. Yet we also seem to feel we have a missionary duty to stop anything labeled Communist wherever it appears. With such conflicting, if not contradictory, policies it's no wonder our country gets itself into trouble.

Sydney Smith, a British theologian of the last century, stated our predicament very well in one sentence when he said, "Errors to be dangerous must have a great deal of truth mingled with them." We have allowed ourselves to be convinced of the "rightness" of incompatible ideas because there was so much truth mingled with them. I think the time has come to reexamine those ideas to see that they don't lead us to even more serious trouble.

And as I fly back to Washington tonight I'm going to be thinking of the prayer which that wonderful organization, Alcoholics Anonymous, teaches to its members; it might teach this nation something too:

> *Oh Lord, give us the strength to change the*
> *things which can be changed;*
> *The courage to accept the things which cannot be*
> *changed,*
> *And the wisdom to know the difference.*

ASSESSMENT IN VIETNAM[5]

MIKE MANSFIELD[6]

Raymond Moley once remarked that a "major contribution of the academic man in politics is a certain detachment from pure expediency. Though he has no monopoly on idealism, he is able to contribute historical and philosophic perspective to political decision making." Some of our most articulate and knowledgeably dedicated senators are former professors: Wayne Morse, George McGovern, Gale McGee, J. W. Fulbright, Eugene McCarthy, and Mike Mansfield. And the number of academic people who serve as consultants and researchers is large. Estimates by Thomas L. Hughes, Director of Intelligence and Research in the United States Department of State, put the academics in the Cambridge area alone at five thousand.

That there has long been a lingering suspicion in some people's minds about the wisdom of the marriage of politics and teaching, no one would deny. In an address at Hamilton College, Clinton, New York, in late 1965, Thomas L. Hughes reflected on an event in 404 B.C.

> [When] some energetic young men took over the government of Athens several of them had been students at a local academy of political science. The idea occurred to them to appoint a distinguished professor of politics to office. He accepted. His name was Plato. The government—that of Critias and the Thirty Tyrants—was one of the worst Athens has had, before or since. The professor lasted only a few months. An outraged city booted the government out of office. Ever since there has been a certain magnetic tension between scholars and statesmen. . . .

But conditions are different now. Presidents from Franklin D. Roosevelt on have, with varying measures of confidence, turned to the intellectuals for counsel and assistance in the management of public affairs. One of the powerful elected officials whose advice is constantly sought and whose voice in governmental matters is invariably strong is Mike Mansfield, Democratic senator from Montana since 1952, and majority leader in the

[5] Indiana University, Bloomington, February 23, 1968. Text furnished by Senator Mansfield, with permission for this reprint.

[6] For biographical note, see Appendix.

Senate since 1961. A member of the Foreign Relations Committee, he speaks authoritatively in and out of Congress on the critical issues which are in the forefront of national attention. Careful of statement, severely disciplined in his utterance, the former professor of history and political science at Montana State University has pleaded tirelessly in recent years for a resolution of the Vietnam war. Some two years ago he issued a detailed report on his visit to South Vietnam, and pressed for negotiations to end the war. Within the year he has urged that talks be arranged between Saigon and the National Liberation Front. In a speech at the University of Maine on February 11, 1968, he remarked that from the beginning,

> it was not an American responsibility and it is not now an American responsibility to win a victory for any particular Vietnamese group, or to defeat any particular Vietnamese group. It was not then and it is not now an American function to insure that any political structure shall be enshrined over the smoldering ruins of a devastated Vietnam. Even if we could, we should not seek to synthesize a government or system for South Vietnam. That is not the responsibility of the American military command, the American economists and the American political scientists who are gathered in Saigon or elsewhere. That is a responsibility which can only be exercised by the Vietnamese people themselves. The sooner that the limits of our commitment are recognized by all directly concerned, therefore, the better for all concerned.

In late 1967 before the Senate Foreign Relations Committee, Senator Mansfield pressed for a resolution that would induce the Administration to present the Vietnam issue to the United Nations. During the discussions, Ambassador Goldberg intimated that the Administration might accede to Vietcong participation in talks if the UN took the lead in suggesting it.

In the address reprinted below, which was delivered at Indiana University on February 23, 1968, Senator Mansfield repeated his plea for an end of our military engagement. Even more particularly, he reflected on the Pueblo incident and urged active UN involvement in arriving at a solution of the crises in Vietnam and Korea:

> We should and can make clear, by procedural vote, that we are willing to submit this question of Vietnam to the Security Council. We should and can make clear, by procedural vote, that we are prepared to invite any nation or group which is of relevance to a settlement, including Hanoi and

the NLF and China, to participate in a face-to-face discussion of the war. We should and can make clear, by procedural vote, that if the emotions kindled by the conflict render undesirable a meeting of the Security Council in New York, we are prepared to see the Council meet in Geneva or anywhere else, as provided for by the Charter. In short, we should and can make clear, by votes, that we are willing to follow the UN path to peace.

It would seem, he continued,

that among the fifteen member nations of the Security Council, there ought to be found at least the required nine votes to respond to an initiative of the United States, calling for a UN effort to open the door to a settlement in Vietnam.

The trouble in Korea, he declared,

coming on top of Vietnam, indicates the hydra-headed potential of war on the Asian continent. The new and dangerous confrontation in the former suggests the urgency of ending the conflict on an honorable basis in the latter. I do not know what the prospect for peace may be by way of the UN approach which has been suggested. Obviously, a UN approach cannot be any less effective than the countless other approaches which have already been attempted without success. On the other hand, it may not be any more effective.

With peace talks between Hanoi and Washington underway, the hope for a solution of the conflict is brightening. The words of men like Senator Mansfield have doubtless contributed importantly to the realization of that prospect.

The struggle in Vietnam has turned grim, pitiless, and devastating. The casualty figures are staggering. The physical damage is enormous. Men, women, children, soldiers, guerrillas, weapons, machines, cities, towns, and villages—all are thrown together in an inferno of destruction.

It is not surprising that the situation has been interpreted in some quarters as approaching some sort of climax. It may well be, as has been suggested, the beginning of the end. The question is what beginning and what end? Peace by military victory? Peace by negotiations? With whom? For what? There is no certainty at this point as to what will emerge in Vietnam, or for that matter, whether the end of this war is to be found in Vietnam.

I have no desire, therefore, to indulge, today, in what has become a kind of parlor game called Who's Winning in Vietnam? It is offensive to me, as I know it must be to you, to hear this deadly conflict treated as some sort of athletic contest. The lives of too many young Americans are on the line in Vietnam. Too many bewildered men and women and children are being burnt, bloodied and broken by this war. Too much is in ruins. Too many lie dead. Vietnam is not a game. There can be no winners; there are only losers and the longer the war persists the greater are the losses for all concerned.

The tragedy of Vietnam constrains us all to great sobriety in discussion. There is little point in speculating on the current clashes—who is winning and who is not, or what is being won and what is not. The need is to try to define accurately the character of the present tragedy and, in that way, hopefully, to see more clearly what the interests of this nation will require in the days ahead.

In this respect, seldom has a problem presented greater difficulties than Vietnam and seldom has the need for a solution been greater. A restoration of peace is imperative for the welfare of the people of Vietnam; they have been fought over for so long that, in the millions, they are torn from their ancestral places seeking refuge where there is no refuge. For us, too, an honorable solution is of the utmost urgency. The war in Vietnam has been deeply divisive in its effects on this nation. It has diverted energy and resources from the great needs of our own society. The vast difficulties of the urban areas, for example, cry out for attention, but the cry is barely heard above the din of the distant conflict.

The nation's economic equilibrium is in danger of being thrown out of kilter by the immense demands of the war. In this connection, we have already suffered a significant degree of inflation. Furthermore, we are confronted with what can only be called the embarrassment of having to discourage the travel of Americans abroad, because of difficulties which the war and other foreign commitments have introduced into the nation's balance of payments.

In our relations with the rest of the world, the war in Vietnam has placed formidable blocks in the way of further progress in international cooperation. It has brought in its wake new threats to the stability of peace, as in the case of the U.S.S. Pueblo incident which may be but the precursor of others. In these pinpoints of instability, moreover, there are ever-present threats to the frail defenses of the world against nuclear catastrophe.

We did not arrive at this situation overnight. Our involvement in Vietnam is not newborn. If we are at a crossroads, today, it is but one in a chain of crossroads which extends backwards for many years. There comes to mind, for example, the moment of the French collapse and the Geneva Conferences of 1954; the assassination of President Ngo Dinh Diem in 1963 and the replacement of civilian government in Saigon by a series of unstable regimes, drawn ever more steadily from military sources, ever more dependent on the United States. Finally, there comes to mind the Tonkin Bay incident and the large-scale direct military engagement of the United States thereafter in the war in Vietnam.

In retrospect it is apparent that at each of these crossroads the American military involvement has deepened. It is also apparent that the successive increases in military commitment have led, so far, not to peace, but rather to an increase in countermilitary commitment. At the end of 1965, five Senators including myself visited Vietnam. In a report made public at the conclusion of our study, we stated that we had found that this nation's military effort was ". . . pressing against a military situation which is, in effect, open ended. How open is dependent on the extent to which North Vietnam and its supporters are willing and able to meet increased force by increased force."

How open the war? How able and willing the opposing forces to meet increased force by increased force?

Our armed forces in Vietnam have increased from 23,000 at the beginning of 1965 to more than half a million today. The bombing of North Vietnam by air and sea has grown from specific retaliation for specific Vietcong acts of offense against our forces into the most systematic air and naval bombardment since World War II. The tonnage of explosives which has fallen upon Vietnam is already higher than in Korea, or, for that matter, in the entire Pacific theatre during World War II and probably close to that unloosed in Europe. Moreover, one by one, the limitations on bombing targets in North Vietnam have been removed until a mere handful is all that now stands against indiscriminate destruction of life and property. Indeed, the search for an elusive victory has led some to clamor for that indiscriminate destruction, even to the point of returning Vietnam to the Stone Age.

With escalation has come mounting losses of life on all sides. U.S. casualty lists are already longer in the first five or six weeks of 1968 than they were during the entire year of 1965. In all of 1965, 1,369 Americans were killed. By February 10, this year, 1,674 Americans had already been killed. According to reports issued in Saigon on yesterday, 543 additional Americans were killed in the last seven days, the highest weekly total of the war. The over-all figures now stand at 18,239 deaths and the wounded total 112,469. Among the opposing forces, of course, there are reports of astronomical increases in men killed, taken prisoner, or deserting.

I cite these gruesome figures to indicate the immense growth in the scope of the conflict, particularly as it has involved the United States. I find it most inappropriate that this effort and these great sacrifices are, in effect, called inadequate in some quarters. The fact is that, short of what Prime Minister Wilson has called the "lunacy" of nuclear war, this nation has made a massive military effort in Vietnam. The effort has been made by dedicated Americans, ably led, who have carried out their orders with courage and skill. At this late date, it ought at least to be clear that if the situation in Vietnam has not changed as anticipated, it has not been for want of an extraordinary military effort by the United States. American forces may well have done too much but by no stretch of the imagination can it be said that they have done too little.

Nevertheless, the reality is that the situation has not changed as anticipated. At the time of my last visit to Vietnam in 1965, available estimates indicated that 22 per cent of the population of South Vietnam is under control of the National Liberation Front, 60 per cent under government control, and 18 per cent contested. At the end of last year, the Saigon government was reported as controlling 67 per cent of the population, presumably a gain of 7 per cent. Substantial progress was also reported in the so-called pacification program which had been designed to strengthen and expand Saigon's control over the rural areas.

Then came the wave of attacks against the cities of South Vietnam. One can put whatever interpretation one chooses on these recent clashes. Whatever else they may mean, they bring into question the validity of the measures of military progress which have been used in Saigon. They bring into question the effectiveness of the Saigon political structure, in its present form. They bring into question the pacification program which appears to have gone the route of at least a dozen prior contrived techniques for "winning the people" of Vietnam. They make clear, finally, that the cities of South Vietnam which have heretofore been spared, almost by tacit agreement, have now been drawn fully into the vortex of the war's terrible devastation.

Whatever the outcome of the present battles, the basic military problem is as it has been from the outset. The war remains open-ended and escalation continues to rise with escalation. The National Liberation Front remains omnipresent, from the demilitarized zone at the seventeenth parallel to the southern tip of the peninsula. Its regular forces and guerrillas are obviously steeled to accept great privation and to make enormous sacrifices. The Vietcong remain entrenched and virtually untouched in their traditional strong-holds—the swamps, paddyfields and hamlets of the Mekong Delta—from whence they are able to dispatch forces to re-inforce units which, as is now apparent, honeycomb Saigon and other cities.

It is dangerous to presume that either the forces of the National Liberation Front or North Vietnam are nearing the end of the rope. Actually, Hanoi has committed to the war in the South considerably less than a quarter of the forces of General Vo Nguyen Giap, who is generally credited with masterminding the current military strategy in the South. And beyond North Vietnam lies the untapped manpower of China and the supply sources of both China and the Soviet Union.

These are some of the realities which are not measured by the computers of "progress" in Saigon. These are some of the realities which seem to me to make it imperative to recall the original purposes of the American commitment to South Vietnam. They were, above all else, limited purposes. There is not now and there has never been a mandate to take over a war. The commitment is to support not to supplant.

At the outset, it was not an American responsibility and it is not now an American responsibility to win a victory for any particular group of Vietnamese or to defeat any particu-lar group of Vietnamese. Even if we could, it is not in the interests of this nation to synthesize a political structure for South Vietnam. That is not and ought not ever to become the function of the American military command, the Ameri-can economists, administrators, diplomats, political scientists, aid officials, and others who are gathered in Vietnam. The sooner that the limits of our commitment are understood by all directly concerned the better for all concerned.

It is time to recognize that our immense effort has already gone a long way to alter the character of what was once an inner struggle among Vietnamese. It is also time to recognize that whatever we may do, the future of Vietnam depends not on us but on the Vietnamese themselves. It is their country; they live in it. They will be living in it long after we are gone from it.

Our responsibility is to sustain, not to submerge. To strip the Vietnamese struggle of its Vietnamese character, to convert it into a war to be won or lost by this nation, is to detract from its relevance both to the people of Vietnam and to the people of the United States. To do so is to consolidate an American involvement on the Southeast Asian mainland of indefinite duration and obscure purposes whose terminus is not visible—not in Vietnam, not in Laos, or in Cambodia. Indeed, it may well be an involvement which is without exit except in World War III.

This nation is deeply committed in South Vietnam but let us not make the mistake of interpreting that commitment as compelling us—in the name of victory or whatever—to see to it that every last member of the NLF [National Liberation Front] is either dulled, dead, captive, or in flight. That course leads not to an ending but to an endless succession of violent beginnings.

An inextricable involvement of American forces in Vietnam may meet the needs of some but it accords neither with the interests of the United States or the people of Vietnam. In this connection, President Johnson has repeatedly stated that this nation's objective is ". . . only that the people of South Vietnam be allowed to guide their own country in their own way." He has stated that he is willing to move at any time in negotiations which might bring about that result. He has stated that we are prepared to move out lock, stock, and barrel in a matter of months after a satisfactory settlement is achieved.

It should be clear, therefore, to all concerned—Americans and Vietnamese in Washington, in Saigon, and in Hanoi and to whomever, wherever—that that is the accurate measure of this nation's commitment. There is no obligation to continue to pour out the blood and resources of this nation until South Vietnam is made safe for one Vietnamese faction or

another. On the contrary, there is an obligation to the people
of the United States to conserve that blood and those resources and, to the people of Vietnam, there is an obligation
to avoid the destruction of their land and society even in
the name of saving them.

Indeed, in my judgment, there is now little prospect of
meeting these deep obligations to the people of this nation
and to the people of Vietnam unless there is a prompt cessation of the bloodletting and the negotiation of an honorable
settlement. For that reason, every possibility of peace must
continue to be explored fully and with the utmost urgency.

The North Vietnamese have stated that they will open
negotiations if the bombing of the North is discontinued. In
that connection, it should be noted, first, that the bombing
has not achieved the purposes for which it was sanctioned.
The bombing has not stopped the movement of men and
supplies into the South; on the contrary, the routes of infiltration carry a heavier traffic than ever before and the traffic
includes ever more sophisticated weapons. The bombing has
done little, if anything, for the morale of the people of South
Vietnam and such indications as there are, suggest that it
has done a great deal to strengthen the determination of the
people of North Vietnam. Finally, the bombing has not yet
brought Hanoi to the conference table, as a suspension, now,
probably will. In short, the bombing of the North has added
a vast dimension to the war. It has raised the cost of the war
in lives and resources—American and other—but it has not
brought closer—so far as can be seen—an honorable end to
the conflict.

It is in this context that I have endorsed a proposal to
confine the bombing to the infiltration routes at the seventeenth parallel. It may be that in this proposal, which was
advanced initially by Senator Cooper of Kentucky—a former
Ambassador to India—may be found a first step to peace. I
am frank to state, however, that while there is reason to
expect an opening of negotiations if the bombing of the
North is curbed, it is not at all certain that negotiations, in

turn, will bring the conflict to an honorable conclusion. Negotiations may be futile; they may fail. In the end, they may prove no more effective, than military escalation has proved to be, in bringing this war to an acceptable end.

Indeed, it is not likely that negotiations will be fruitful at this time if the conflict is defined as a simple, clear-cut case of aggression on the part of the North against the South or as some sort of final test which has pitted the forces of freedom in Vietnam in a showdown against communism. The reality in Vietnam is far more complex, both in the relationships which exist between North and South Vietnam and among the various groups and elements within South Vietnam. How complex, for example, is indicated by the composition of the present government in Saigon. It is based almost entirely upon a military faction and most of its principals are not Southern Vietnamese but Northern Vietnamese. They are clearly not the whole coin of political leadership in South Vietnam. There are other sources of indigenous leadership, other groups which are without significant voice in the present Southern political structure.

It would be an advance towards peace, in my judgment, if the door to reconciliation could be opened among South Vietnamese of all political inclinations. If that is not to be, however, I cannot see that the diplomacy of this nation must remain hog-tied by the inflexibility of others. The responsibilities which are owed to the people of this nation and Vietnam urge the seeking of an honorable peace, wherever and however it may be found and regardless of who may be willing to join in the search.

It is possible that the divergent fears and interests which are involved—directly and indirectly—in the Vietnamese conflict may still be reconcilable on the basis of the Geneva Accords of 1954 and 1962. These agreements might still provide a framework for determining, in peace, the future relationship of the two parts of Vietnam and for guaranteeing the neutralization of Vietnam and of Indochina. A reactivation of the Geneva Conference, therefore, by the co-chairmen

—the United Kingdom and the Soviet Union—is clearly desirable. Geneva, however, is not necessarily the only beacon of peace and, in any event, it has yet to be lit. If the Secretary-General of the United Nations, a group of Asian nations, European nations, African nations, Communist nations or any combination thereof were prepared and able to convene a peace conference, those approaches, too, are obviously worthy of every consideration.

The Senate voted a resolution on November 30th last, urging that Vietnam be brought actively before the Security Council of the United Nations. The proposal was for a direct approach to the problem by means of the open processes of the UN Charter.

At the very least, an initiative in the UN Security Council would help to clarify the significance of the words of peace which are raised on all sides. At the very least, it could help to emphasize this nation's readiness to take its chances on a peaceful settlement of the conflict in accord with the world-sanctioned premises of the Charter.

In my judgment, we should and can make clear, by procedural vote, that we are willing to submit this question of Vietnam to the Security Council. We should and can make clear, by procedural vote, that we are prepared to invite any nation or group which is of relevance to a settlement, including Hanoi and the NLF and China, to participate in a face-to-face discussion of the war. We should and can make clear, by procedural vote, that if the emotions kindled by the conflict render undesirable a meeting of the Security Council in New York, we are prepared to see the Council meet in Geneva or anywhere else, as provided for by the Charter. In short, we should and can make clear, by votes, that we are willing to follow the UN path to peace.

It would seem that among the fifteen member nations of the Security Council, there ought to be found at least the required nine votes to respond to an initiative of the United States, calling for a UN effort to open the door to a settlement in Vietnam.

Nevertheless, if such is not the case, it seems desirable to know now, by formal and open test, win or lose, who is willing and who is unwilling to confront the issue of peace in Vietnam before the bar of the world. May I say that it does no service to the United Nations to shrink from bringing before it a situation which involves its fundamental reason for being.

On this point, I would note, too, that the members of the UN ought not to overlook the obligations of the organization in connection with the rising tensions in Korea. The UN has been involved—deeply involved—for two decades in Korea. It was with the sanction of the UN that this nation carried the main burden of the war which was fought in Korea. It was with UN guidance that the truce in Korea was achieved. It is still within the competence of the UN to deal with the unresolved questions of Korea, and, in particular, when they pose threats of renewed war.

Insofar as this nation's unilateral responsibilities respecting Korea are concerned, the firm restraint which President Johnson has exercised from the outset in the Pueblo affair, in my judgment, has set a wise course. The question is being pursued quietly at the Panmunjom truce site in discussions between our representatives and those of North Korea. Third-party channels are also being explored. In short, the effort at this time is to seek by diplomacy the release of the crewmen alive—I repeat, alive. It is a prudent course in what is, at best, a delicate and dangerous situation and it deserves every support.

Talks at Panmunjom and the search for third-party intercession, however, do not begin to exhaust the possibilities of solution. If these efforts do not bear fruit, other options may also be available. The President has already had the matter raised at the UN Security Council by Ambassador Goldberg. If necessary, it can and should be pressed anew in that forum. It may be feasible, thereby, to seek an impartial investigation, arbitration or mediation of the dispute or a presentation of the entire matter to the World Court.

Whatever the specific recourse, in my judgment, the efforts to find a peaceful settlement of the Pueblo affair are attuned to this nation's interest. What matters, first, is the safe release of the crewmen. What matters most is the substance not the shadow of this nation's interests.

The flare-up in Korea, coming on top of Vietnam, indicates the hydra-headed potential of war on the Asian continent. The new and dangerous confrontation in the former suggests the urgency of ending the conflict on an honorable basis in the latter. I do not know what the prospect for peace may be by way of the UN approach which has been suggested. Obviously, a UN approach cannot be any less effective than the countless other approaches which have already been attempted without success. On the other hand, it may not be any more effective.

In any event, somewhere, somehow, there must be the beginnings of a negotiated settlement. Until it is found, the fires of conflict will blaze ever more fiercely in Vietnam; the arc of war's wreckage will continue to open on the continent of Asia. And if the fires burn out of control to World War III, what nation will then claim the victory? Indeed, what nation will be left to claim it?

REMARKS TO THE NATION[7]

LYNDON B. JOHNSON[8]

Any speaker who manages to develop one dramatic idea in a given address ordinarily considers himself fortunate. If he hits upon two stunning ideas, the statement partakes of a rhetorical shockwave. President Johnson shaped such a formula on March 31, 1968, in a nationally televised address from Washington, D.C. In considerable detail, he announced the cessation of bombing of much of North Vietnam. And, then, in an electrifying remark, he said: "I shall not seek, and I will not accept, the nomination of my Party for another term as your President." Before the echo of the words had faded, new political plans and maneuvers began to take shape, rhetorical stratagems of the principal contenders for the nomination—Senators Eugene McCarthy and Robert F. Kennedy—underwent change, and the Republicans took a fresh look at the realities posed by a change in top administration.

Indications of change in public attitude toward the President were immediately evident. His address had a genuinely moving quality, a dramatic fervor which invariably accompanies an announcement of withdrawal from a position of high authority. Some of the acerbic criticism, especially of his Vietnam policy, was eased momentarily in the hopeful prospect that an unpopular war was finally moving toward the first stages of settlement. By removing himself from the political context of the coming elections, and by dedicating himself more fully to the urgent business of peace, he helped to create—so many believed—a new climate in which to hammer out a solution to the dilemmas in Southeast Asia. "The President's speech," commented the Minneapolis *Tribune*, "was statesmanship on a plane commensurate with the traditions and ideals associated with the nation's highest office."

But man's conduct is subject to strange ironies. Soon after the President's speech, Tom Wicker of the New York *Times* remarked that it was Mr. Johnson's fate to move "Americans most at the first and last"—when he received the overwhelming mandate from the people in 1964 and when he bowed out of the scene in 1968. Perhaps this is, as Wicker observed, the ultimate irony: "Lyn-

[7] The White House, Washington, D.C., March 31, 1968. Text furnished by the office of the Press Secretary to the President.

[8] For biographical note, see Appendix.

don Johnson came into office seeking a great society in America and found instead an ugly little war that consumed him."

Students of public address will note the parallels between President Johnson's address of March 31 and President Truman's address of March 29, 1952, when he too said he would "not accept a renomination." Both men were at once the leaders and victims of an Asian conflict; both were targets of heavy criticism, though by contrast the shafts aimed at Mr. Truman were merely love darts.

Editorial comment and mail response to President Johnson's speech were heavy. Within three or four days, some 13,000 letters and 4,000 telegrams poured into the White House. More important, however, was the unrecorded impression upon an estimated 77 million viewers of a kind of personal drama that revealed a man in the act of changing the pattern of his life. "If the role of live television was ever in doubt," wrote Jack Gould, television editor of the New York *Times,* "President Johnson's surprise announcement not to seek renomination affirmed the stunning and matchless impact of the TV medium when it allows a viewer to share in the making of history."

Good evening, my fellow Americans.

Tonight I want to speak to you of peace in Vietnam and Southeast Asia.

No other question so preoccupies our people. No other dream so absorbs the 250 million human beings who live in that part of the world. No other goal motivates American policy in Southeast Asia.

For years, representatives of our government and others have traveled the world—seeking to find a basis for peace talks.

Since last September, they have carried the offer that I made public at San Antonio.

That offer was this:

That the United States would stop its bombardment of North Vietnam when that would lead promptly to productive discussions—and that we would assume that North Vietnam would not take military advantage of our restraint.

Hanoi denounced this offer, both privately and publicly. Even while the search for peace was going on, North Vietnam rushed their preparations for a savage assault on the people, the government, and the allies of South Vietnam.

Their attack—during the Tet holidays—failed to achieve its principal objectives.

It did not collapse the elected government of South Vietnam or shatter its army—as the Communists had hoped.

It did not produce a "general uprising" among the people of the cities as they had predicted.

The Communists were unable to maintain control of any of the more than thirty cities that they attacked. And they took very heavy casualties.

But they did compel the South Vietnamese and their allies to move certain forces from the countryside, into the cities.

They caused widespread disruption and suffering. Their attacks, and the battles that followed, made refugees of half a million human beings.

The Communists may renew their attack any day.

They are, it appears, trying to make 1968 the year of decision in South Vietnam—the year that brings, if not final victory or defeat, at least a turning point in the struggle.

This much is clear:

If they do mount another round of heavy attacks, they will not succeed in destroying the fighting power of South Vietnam and its allies.

But tragically, this is also clear: many men—on both sides of the struggle—will be lost. A nation that has already suffered twenty years of warfare will suffer once again. Armies on both sides will take new casualties. And the war will go on.

There is no need for this to be so.

There is no need to delay the talks that could bring an end to this long and this bloody war.

Tonight, I renew the offer I made last August—to stop the bombardment of North Vietnam. We ask that talks begin promptly, that they be serious talks on the substance of peace. We assume that during those talks Hanoi will not take advantage of our restraint.

We are prepared to move immediately toward peace through negotiations.

So, tonight, in the hope that this action will lead to early talks, I am taking the first step to deescalate the conflict. We are reducing—substantially reducing—the present level of hostilities.

And we are doing so unilaterally, and at once.

Tonight, I have ordered our aircraft and our naval vessels to make no attacks on North Vietnam, except in the area north of the Demilitarized Zone where the continuing enemy build-up directly threatens allied forward positions and where the movements of their troops and supplies are clearly related to that threat.

The area in which we are stopping our attacks includes almost 90 per cent of North Vietnam's population, and most of its territory. Thus there will be no attacks around the principal populated areas, or in the food-producing areas of North Vietnam.

Even this very limited bombing of the North could come to an early end—if our restraint is matched by restraint in Hanoi. But I cannot in good conscience stop all bombing so long as to do so would immediately and directly endanger the lives of our men and our allies. Whether a complete bombing halt becomes possible in the future will be determined by events.

Our purpose in this action is to bring about a reduction in the level of violence that now exists.

It is to save the lives of brave men—and to save the lives of innocent women and children. It is to permit the contending forces to move closer to a political settlement.

And tonight, I call upon the United Kingdom and I call upon the Soviet Union—as co-chairmen of the Geneva Conferences, and as permanent members of the United Nations Security Council—to do all they can to move from the unilateral act of deescalation that I have just announced toward genuine peace in Southeast Asia.

Now, as in the past, the United States is ready to send its representatives to any forum, at any time, to discuss the means of bringing this ugly war to an end.

I am designating one of our most distinguished Americans, Ambassador Averell Harriman, as my personal representative for such talks. In addition, I have asked Ambassador Llewellyn Thompson, who returned from Moscow for consultation, to be available to join Ambassador Harriman at Geneva or any other suitable place—just as soon as Hanoi agrees to a conference.

I call upon President Ho Chi Minh to respond positively, and favorably, to this new step toward peace.

But if peace does not come now through negotiations, it will come when Hanoi understands that our common resolve is unshakable, and our common strength is invincible.

Tonight, we and the other allied nations are contributing 600,000 fighting men to assist 700,000 South Vietnamese troops in defending their little country.

Our presence there has always rested on this basic belief: the main burden of preserving their freedom must be carried out by them—by the South Vietnamese themselves.

We and our allies can only help to provide a shield—behind which the people of South Vietnam can survive and can grow and develop. On their efforts—on their determination and resourcefulness—the outcome will ultimately depend.

That small, beleaguered nation has suffered terrible punishment for more than twenty years.

I pay tribute once again tonight to the great courage and endurance of its people. South Vietnam supports armed forces tonight of almost 700,000 men—and I call your attention to the fact that that is the equivalent of more than 10 million in our own population. Its people maintain their firm determination to be free of domination by the North.

There has been substantial progress, I think, in building a durable government during these last three years. The South Vietnam of 1965 could not have survived the enemy's

Tet offensive of 1968. The elected government of South Vietnam survived that attack—and is rapidly repairing the devastation that it wrought.

The South Vietnamese know that further efforts are going to be required:

to expand their own armed forces

to move back into the countryside as quickly as possible

to increase their taxes

to select the very best men that they have for civilian and military responsibility

to achieve a new unity within their constitutional government

and to include in the national effort all of those groups who wish to preserve South Vietnam's control over its own destiny

Last week President Thieu ordered the mobilization of 135,000 additional South Vietnamese. He plans to reach—as soon as possible—a total military strength of more than 800,000 men.

To achieve this, the government of South Vietnam started the drafting of nineteen-year-olds on March 1st. On May 1st, the Government will begin the drafting of eighteen-year-olds.

Last month 10,000 men volunteered for military service —that was two and a half times the number of volunteers during the same month last year. Since the middle of January more than 48,000 South Vietnamese have joined the armed forces—and nearly half of them volunteered to do so.

All men in the South Vietnamese armed forces have had their tours of duty extended for the duration of the war, and reserves are now being called up for immediate active duty.

President Thieu told his people last week:

We must make greater efforts and accept more sacrifices because, as I have said many times, this is our country. The existence of our nation is at stake, and this is mainly a Vietnamese responsibility.

He warned his people that a major national effort is required to root out corruption and incompetence at all levels of government.

We applaud this evidence of determination on the part of South Vietnam. Our first priority will be to support their effort.

We shall accelerate the reequipment of South Vietnam's armed forces—in order to meet the enemy's increased fire-power. This will enable them progressively to undertake a larger share of combat operations against the Communist invaders.

On many occasions I have told the American people that we would send to Vietnam those forces that are required to accomplish our mission there. So, with that as our guide, we have previously authorized a force level of approximately 525,000.

Some weeks ago—to help meet the enemy's new offensive —we sent to Vietnam about 11,000 additional Marine and airborne troops. They were deployed by air in forty-eight hours, on an emergency basis. But the artillery, tank, aircraft, and other units that were needed to work with and support these infantry troops in combat could not accompany them on that short notice.

In order that these forces may reach maximum combat effectiveness, the Joint Chiefs of Staff have recommended to me that we should prepare to send—during the next five months—support troops totaling approximately 13,500 men.

A portion of these men will be made available from our active forces. The balance will come from Reserve component units which will be called up for service.

The actions that we have taken since the beginning of the year
      to reequip the South Vietnamese forces
      to meet our responsibilities in Korea, as well as our responsibilities in Vietnam
      to meet price increases and the cost of activating and deploying reserve forces
      to replace helicopters and provide the other military supplies we need

—all of these actions are going to require additional expenditures.

The tentative estimate of those additional expenditures is $2.5 billion in this fiscal year, and $2.6 billion in the next fiscal year.

These projected increases will bring into sharper focus the nation's need for immediate action: action to protect the prosperity of the American people and to protect the strength and the stability of our American dollar.

On many occasions I have pointed out that, without a tax bill or decreased expenditures, next year's deficit would again be around $20 billion. I have emphasized the need to set strict priorities in our spending. I have stressed that failure to act and to act promptly and decisively would raise very strong doubt throughout the world about America's willingness to keep its financial house in order.

Yet Congress has not acted. And tonight we face the sharpest financial threat in the postwar era—a threat to the dollar's role as the keystone of international trade and finance in the world.

Last week, at the monetary conference in Stockholm, the major industrial countries decided to take a big step toward creating a new international monetary asset that will strengthen the international monetary system. I am very proud of the very able work done by Secretary Fowler and Chairman Martin of the Federal Reserve Board.

But to make this system work the United States just must bring its balance of payments to—or very close to—equilibrium. We must have a responsible fiscal policy in this country. The passage of a tax bill now, together with expenditure control that the Congress may desire and dictate, is absolutely necessary to protect this nation's security, to continue our prosperity, and to meet the needs of our people.

What is at stake is seven years of unparalleled prosperity —in those seven years, the real income of the average American—after taxes—rose by almost 30 per cent, a gain as large as that of the entire preceding nineteen years.

So the steps that we must take to convince the world are exactly the steps we must take to sustain our own economic strength here at home. In the past eight months, prices and interest rates have risen because of our inaction.

We must, therefore, now do everything we can to move from debate to action—from talking to voting. There is, I believe—I hope there is—in both houses of the Congress—a growing sense of urgency that this situation just must be acted upon and must be corrected.

My budget in January was, we thought, a tight one. It fully reflected our evaluation of most of the demanding needs of this nation.

But in these budgetary matters, the President does not decide alone. The Congress has the power and the duty to determine appropriations and taxes.

The Congress is now considering our proposals and they are considering reductions in the budget that we submitted.

As part of a program of fiscal restraint that includes the tax surcharge, I shall approve appropriate reductions in the January budget when and if Congress so decides that that should be done.

One thing is unmistakably clear, however: our deficit just must be reduced. Failure to act could bring on conditions that would strike hardest at those people that all of us are trying so hard to help.

These times call for prudence in this land of plenty. I believe that we have the character to provide it, and tonight I plead with the Congress and with the people to act promptly to serve the national interest, and thereby serve all of our people.

Now let me give you my estimate of the chances for peace:

the peace that will one day stop the bloodshed in South Vietnam;

that all the Vietnamese people will be permitted to rebuild and develop their land;

that will permit us to turn more fully to our own tasks here at home.

I cannot promise that the initiative that I have announced tonight will be completely successful in achieving peace any more than the thirty others that we have undertaken and agreed to in recent years.

But it is our fervent hope that North Vietnam, after years of fighting that has left the issue unresolved, will now cease its efforts to achieve a military victory and will join with us in moving toward the peace table.

And there may come a time when South Vietnamese—on both sides—are able to work out a way to settle their own differences by free political choice rather than by war.

As Hanoi considers its course, it should be in no doubt of our intentions. It must not miscalculate the pressures within our democracy in this election year.

We have no intention of widening this war.

But the United States will never accept a fake solution to this long and arduous struggle and call it peace.

No one can foretell the precise terms of an eventual settlement.

Our objective in South Vietnam has never been the annihilation of the enemy. It has been to bring about a recognition in Hanoi that its objective—taking over the South by force—could not be achieved.

We think that peace can be based on the Geneva Accords of 1954—under political conditions that permit the South Vietnamese—all the South Vietnamese—to chart their course free of any outside domination or interference, from us or from anyone else.

So tonight I reaffirm the pledge that we made at Manila —that we are prepared to withdraw our forces from South Vietnam as the other side withdraws its forces to the North, stops the infiltration, and the level of violence thus subsides.

Our goal of peace and self-determination in Vietnam is directly related to the future of all of Southeast Asia—where much has happened to inspire confidence during the past ten years. We have done all that we knew how to do to contribute and to help build that confidence.

A number of its nations have shown what can be accomplished under conditions of security. Since 1966 Indonesia, the fifth largest nation in all the world, with a population of more than 100 million people, has had a government that is dedicated to peace with its neighbors and improved conditions for its own people. Political and economic cooperation between nations has grown rapidly.

I think every American can take a great deal of pride in the role that we have played in bringing this about in Southeast Asia. We shall rightly judge—as responsible Southeast Asians themselves do—that the progress of the past three years would have been far less likely—if not completely impossible—if America's sons and others had not made their stand in Vietnam.

At Johns Hopkins University, about three years ago, I announced that the United States would take part in the great work of developing Southeast Asia, including the Mekong Valley—for all the people of that region. Our determination to help build a better land—a better land for men on both sides of the present conflict—has not diminished in the least. Indeed, the ravages of war, I think, have made it more urgent than ever.

So, I repeat on behalf of the United States again tonight what I said at Johns Hopkins—that North Vietnam could take its place in this common effort just as soon as peace comes.

Over time, a wider framework of peace and security in Southeast Asia may become possible. The new cooperation of the nations in the area could be a foundation-stone. Certainly friendship with the nations of such a Southeast Asia is what the United States seeks—and that is all that the United States seeks.

One day, my fellow citizens, there will be peace in Southeast Asia.

It will come because the people of Southeast Asia want it —those whose armies are at war tonight, and those who, though threatened, have thus far been spared.

Peace will come because Asians were willing to work for it—and to sacrifice for it—and to die by the thousands for it.

But let it never be forgotten: peace will come also because America sent her sons to help secure it.

It has not been easy—far from it. During the past four and a half years, it has been my fate and my responsibility to be commander-in-chief. I have lived—daily and nightly—with the cost of this war. I know the pain that it has inflicted. I know perhaps better than anyone the misgivings that it has aroused.

Throughout this entire, long period, I have been sustained by a single principle: that what we are doing now, in Vietnam, is vital not only to the security of Southeast Asia, but it is vital to the security of every American.

Surely we have treaties which we must respect. Surely we have commitments that we are going to keep. Resolutions of the Congress testify to the need to resist aggression in the world and in Southeast Asia.

But the heart of our involvement in South Vietnam— under three Presidents, three separate Administrations—has always been America's own security.

And the larger purpose of our involvement has always been to help the nations of Southeast Asia become independent and stand alone, self-sustaining as members of a great world community—at peace with themselves, and at peace with all others.

With such an Asia, our country—and the world—will be far more secure than it is tonight.

I believe that a peaceful Asia is far nearer to reality, because of what America has done in Vietnam. I believe that the men who endure the dangers of battle—fighting there for us tonight—are helping the entire world avoid far greater conflicts, far wider wars, far more destruction, than this one.

The peace that will bring them home some day will come. Tonight I have offered the first in what I hope will be a series of mutual moves toward peace.

I pray that it will not be rejected by the leaders of North Vietnam. I pray that they will accept it as a means by which the sacrifices of their own people may be ended. And I ask your help and your support, my fellow citizens, for this effort to reach across the battlefield toward an early peace.

Finally, my fellow Americans, let me say this:

Of those to whom much is given, much is asked. I cannot say and no man could say that no more will be asked of us.

Yet, I believe that now, no less than when the decade began, this generation of Americans is willing to pay any price, bear any burden, meet any hardship, support any friend, oppose any foe, to assure the survival and the success of liberty.

Since those words were spoken by John F. Kennedy, the people of America have kept that compact with mankind's noblest cause.

And we shall continue to keep it.

Yet, I believe that we must always be mindful of this one thing, whatever the trials and the tests ahead. The ultimate strength of our country and our cause will lie not in powerful weapons or infinite resources or boundless wealth, but will lie in the unity of our people.

This, I believe very deeply.

Throughout my entire public career I have followed the personal philosophy that I am a free man, an American, a public servant and a member of my Party, in that order always and only.

For thirty-seven years in the service of our nation, first as a Congressman, as a Senator and as Vice President and now as your President, I have put the unity of the people first. I have put it ahead of any divisive partisanship.

And in these times as in times before, it is true that a house divided against itself by the spirit of faction, of party, of region, of religion, of race, is a house that cannot stand.

There is division in the American house now. There is divisiveness among us all tonight. And holding the trust that is mine, as President of all the people, I cannot disregard the peril to the progress of the American people and the hope and the prospect of peace for all peoples.

So, I would ask all Americans, whatever their personal interests or concern, to guard against divisiveness and all its ugly consequences.

Fifty-two months and ten days ago, in a moment of tragedy and trauma, the duties of this office fell upon me. I asked then for your help and God's, that we might continue America on its course, binding up our wounds, healing our history, moving forward in new unity, to clear the American agenda and to keep the American commitment for all of our people.

United we have kept that commitment. United we have enlarged that commitment.

Through all time to come, I think America will be a stronger nation, a more just society, and a land of greater opportunity and fulfillment because of what we have all done together in these years of unparalleled achievement.

Our reward will come in the life of freedom, peace, and hope that our children will enjoy through ages ahead.

What we won when all of our people united just must not now be lost in suspicion, distrust, selfishness, and politics among any of our people.

Believing this as I do, I have concluded that I should not permit the presidency to become involved in the partisan divisions that are developing in this political year.

With America's sons in the fields far away, with America's future under challenge right here at home, with our hopes and the world's hopes for peace in the balance every day, I do not believe that I should devote an hour or a day of my time to any personal partisan causes or to any duties other than the awesome duties of this office—the presidency of your country.

Accordingly, I shall not seek, and I will not accept, the nomination of my Party for another term as your President.

But let men everywhere know, however, that a strong, a confident, and a vigilant America stands ready tonight to seek an honorable peace—and stands ready tonight to defend an honored cause—whatever the price, whatever the burden, whatever the sacrifices that duty may require.

Thank you for listening.

Good night and God bless all of you.

THE URBAN IMPERATIVES

REALITY AND RHETORIC[1]

JOHN V. LINDSAY[2]

In a speech at Palo Alto, California, on February 14, 1968, Donald L. Benedict, executive director of the Community Renewal Society in Chicago said:

> Today in every American city, we stand at a demonic and creative moment. Demonic in the sense that if we do not hear the cry of desperation from the ghetto, the whole fabric of our society may be rent asunder. Creative in the sense that ghetto leadership, with a new sense of confidence in blackness, is reaching out to deal constructively with complex and intricate problems which can lead to the fulfillment of the original American dream of equality and justice for all.

The cry of distress in the city has for many years been loud and clear; but we have failed to listen carefully. With dramatic impact, the urgency has at long last been revealed in all its neglected and ominous dimensions. And, as Mr. Benedict and others have pointed out, the interrelated aspects of the urban crisis have been laid bare: discrimination, inadequate housing, faulty education, welfare deficiencies, stark hunger. Singly and in combination they add up to a shameful formula of despair. Together they make up what John W. Gardner has called "the interlocking clusters of problems of poverty, discrimination and the cities."

Some or all of the actions now proposed or already initiated will, it is hoped, help correct the maladies. The Urban Coalition is at work; domestic Marshall plans are suggested; the White House announced on April 26, 1968, the creation of an Urban Institute; states are considering massive rehabilitation programs; cities are calling for urban bills of rights. But the time is short and the job is big.

[1] Harvard Republican Club and Harvard Student Body, Cambridge, Massachusetts, April 26, 1968. Text furnished by Elizabeth Palay, Administrative Assistant, Press Office, Office of the Mayor of the City of New York, with permission for this reprint.

[2] For biographical note, see Appendix.

If an indelible underscoring of our country's plight was needed, the National Advisory Commission on Civil Disorders furnished it in early 1968 with the publication of its *Report*. This sobering six-hundred-page document set forth a basic conclusion which many thoughtful leaders fear the nation has not taken with proper seriousness: "Our nation is moving toward two societies, one black, one white—separate and unequal."

Among others, Mayor John V. Lindsay of New York City has spoken out against the delay in responding affirmatively and vigorously to the Commission's warning. In an address before the Harvard Republican Club and the Harvard student body (reprinted below) at Cambridge, Massachusetts, on April 20, 1968, he called for accomplishments, not promises. "We must discern and judge the reality, not the rhetoric."

Mr. Lindsay, a Republican member of Congress from 1959 to 1965, and mayor of New York City since 1966, is a highly competent speaker. He appears often before young audiences, and in general fares well. At forty-six, he understands and appreciates the aspirations of the younger generation, and has faith in their ability to help correct the nation's ills. At the same time, however, he counsels against aimless protest which offers no alternatives to present wrongs. Speaking before a one-thousand-student convocation at Brooklyn College on October 27, 1967—in the wake of a short student strike—Mr. Lindsay said:

Those who would rebel against the value and conventions of our society have sound grounds—in logic and in conscience—for doing so. I should remind you, however, of the historic axiom that the rebel who overturns society's conventions assumes the obligation to construct new and better conventions in their place. It is by far the more difficult pursuit.

Mr. Lindsay brings his considerable power of persuasion and personal appeal to bear upon many of the urban and national imperatives of our time. Perhaps the opening lines of Richard Reeves' review of Mr. Lindsay's *Journey into Politics* are more fraught with meaning than a first reading would lead us to believe: "John V. Lindsay is not going to solve the problems of New York City. But he's beginning to convince some people that the problems can be solved."

Any elected official must now face a group like this with more worries and qualms than he would have had two months ago. Speaking to students used to be painless and unworrisome: they couldn't vote you out of office; they judged you more by the sophistication than by the substance of what you said.

Now you've changed all that. You went to New Hampshire and to Wisconsin and stunned the pros. You showed that in 1968 a political organization couldn't deliver the votes if it couldn't convince the people that what it stood for was right. You helped convince an incumbent President that it would not be wise to seek reelection.

And you've put a very high premium on honesty and courage for anyone who would offer to lead you.

Your generation showed the capacity for change and the dimensions of dissent. You picketed, boycotted, and sat in. And this winter you poured your energies and talents into traditional political channels and revolutionized that tradition.

The changes, the uneasiness, the questioning, the sense of critical choices—all these come to us now in part through the work you have done in the civil rights movement. Through action and debate on our involvement in Vietnam. Through your search for new roles and responsibilities for individual participation in the political and academic communities. Let us welcome the questions and the choices. And let us begin to define them and to answer them.

Less than two months ago the National Advisory Commission on Civil Disorders stated: "Our nation is moving toward two societies, one black, one white—separate and unequal." This was a harsh and straightforward assessment. It had been made long ago by the people who live in Harlem, Watts, and Roxbury. It may have surprised them that *this* statement was made without qualification by a group of predominantly white, middle-class Americans.

But many of the nation's political leaders saw it differently. They said it was an exaggeration, or overstatement, or worst of all, that it ignored the significant progress in race relations of the past decade. They squirmed, they quibbled, and they denied that it was so.

Then suddenly the death of Dr. Martin Luther King and its destructive aftermath made the Commission's findings all too real. Many of the same national leaders quickly began to talk about the problem of divisiveness. It was safe now for almost anyone to decry the split in the country and the division between the races.

Did we really need such overwhelming proof as disruptions in 110 additional cities? We had hoped that the Commission's report would end this debate, that the candor of the report would encourage others to adopt a new honesty in their discussions of the problems of the cities and the relationships between the races. But that honesty was not forthcoming.

Nor is it yet clear that we have seen that honesty in response to the killing of Dr. King. How many of the government officials who issued proclamations in city halls and state capitols across the nation on the death of Dr. King had ever bothered to meet with him during his life, to talk with him, speak out for him, or march with him? How many of the corporations that sponsored public memorials after his death had been willing to contribute those funds during his life to his organization or to the cause he championed? And how many of them even now understand that they must either choose to act, or face the terrible costs of inaction.

We face now a new test of our honesty and purpose in confronting the problems described in the Commission Report and exposed in the streets of our nation last week. We will not relieve the tension in the streets of American cities with vague calls for "national reconciliation" or a "searching of men's hearts and minds." This is not the time to design new slogans for America. The promise of this country is clear—the Constitution, the Bill of Rights, the civil rights laws—spell it out unmistakably. This is a time—once and for all—for performance. It is time to make real in our lives the promise that has so long been written in our laws.

Let us be candid and specific about our shortcomings. Twenty-two years ago, in the Employment Act of 1946, Congress established as the policy of this nation the goal of a useful job at a reasonable wage for all who wished to work. In 1964 the official platform of the Democratic party again stated that "Full employment is an end in itself and must be insisted upon as a priority objective." That language is unambiguous—but so is the persistence of chronic and excessive unemployment in every ghetto in this nation. In San Antonio's slums the subemployment rate is 47 per cent; in Boston's slums it is 24 per cent; in New Orleans', it is 45 per cent. Need we ask what any of those men would say if they heard another speech, or another promise, or another pledge? They need jobs. Let us make that our standard.

Let us measure each proposal for America not by its appeal but by its consequences. Let us place it on the streets and study its impact. How will it affect the life of the fifteen-year-old high school dropout at 125th Street and Lenox in Harlem, or the welfare mother with four children on Chicago's Roosevelt Road?

Let us focus on specific legislation—on funding levels, numbers of jobs, salary levels, and on rounding up the votes for passage. The Commission on Civil Disorders recommended specific targets:

The creation of 250,000 new public service jobs this year, and one million over the next three years

The creation of 300,000 new jobs in the private sector this year, and one million such jobs over the next three years

Emergency bills to implement these recommendations have been introduced by Senators Javits of New York and Clark of Pennsylvania. They are languishing in committee. They have failed, like so much other vital urban legislation, to gain the support of the majority of white America.

We must not forget that the crisis of the cities is a crisis for the white man too, and that pressure and fear and bitterness and uncertainty threaten to alienate him too.

Today Americans stand poised for a brief moment undecided, confused, and insecure. There is the danger of stampede toward simple primitive solutions: tanks, guns, firebombs. But these are instruments that cannot work in America, just as they have not worked in Vietnam. Peace cannot be imposed on our cities by force of arms. The social and economic ills that have brought desperation to the ghettos cannot be overcome by military might. We begin to relearn old truths. Violence begets violence. Fear begets fear. A gun in the hands of a policeman aimed at a black teenager will no sooner heal wounds than a brick in the hand of a black man will erase poverty.

There is no simple solution to the disorder of our cities. The problems are complex and so also the solutions. Above all else these are problems of people, and they must be dealt with in human terms and with humane commitments.

If we are to be honestly concerned about the quality of urban life, we must look not only at Harlem and Hough and Lawndale, but also at our Park Avenues, our Lake Shore Drives and our Wilshire Boulevards. These are the streets of white Americans — affluent, defensive and uncertain whether to stay in the city, or to rush to the suburbs to meet the same problems there. For there is no longer any escape for those who would run.

By now it should be clear to every citizen that cities that don't work for black men cannot work for white men. If schools in Woodlawn or Central Square do not work, the price of that failure will be paid by others in West Rodgers Park and Brattle Street in welfare checks and police costs.

But if this nation is not one and equal in its affluence, at least it has become one and equal in its despair. Not only are black and white trapped together in cities that no longer work, they are also trapped together in a senseless struggle overseas whose purpose is not clear. All Americans have heard the nation's highest leaders describe a war in Southeast Asia as consistent with this country's most cherished traditions. Yet we have seen on television a very different conflict. We have been told of success and seen defeat. We have been told of life and seen death. We have been told of tunnels of light and seen graves of darkness. We have been told of freedom and seen repression.

America has been guilty of deception and blindness in our involvement in Vietnam: in our refusal to acknowledge civilian casualties from our bombing of the North; in our unwillingness to admit the existence of the National Liberation Front; and in our stubbornly sanguine assessment of the progress of the military effort and the pacification program. The cost of such self-deception is incalculable. Throughout the world it has undermined the prestige and authority of America because it did not look as if we knew what we were doing or why we were doing it. At home it has forced increasing numbers of citizens to doubt the word of our government—while at the same time the government suggested that those who dissent from its policies are inciting division and guilty of disloyalty.

The price we are paying in lives and in dollars in Vietnam is extremely high. And it is directly related to the cost of inaction in our cities. For the truth, I'm afraid, is that we cannot achieve either the cities or the society we would like as long as we continue the war in Vietnam. We cannot spend more than $24 billion a year in Vietnam and still rebuild our cities. We cannot speak of nonviolence at home when we are displacing, maiming and killing thousands of Asians for the professed purpose of protecting the peace in a land halfway across the world.

These are not healthy signs. These are not the signs of a country that has debated and defined its goals and values at home or in the world, or faced honestly the ambiguity of its position or the limitations of its power.

Just as the Commission report and the death of Martin Luther King demand from all of us some straight talking on the subject of race and the cities, the inconsistencies and the pressures of the Vietnam situation demand some new thinking of all our traditional ideas on foreign policy.

Whatever the answers we find to these questions, whatever the policies we choose, abroad as well as at home, they must be put to the same test: What are the consequences?

We must look to what is accomplished, not what is promised. We must discern and judge the reality, not the rhetoric.

You have made us do just that. The debate of the next seven months must continue on these terms—on the terms that you have helped to set.

I last visited Cambridge in the spring a year ago. Since then your faces have changed. Then there was hestitation and uncertainty. Your causes had few leaders and your actions few consequences. You were only vaguely aware that white and black America were deeply divided. And though increasingly threatened by personal involvement in a war many challenged as immoral, you could plan no course of action that seemed to make much difference.

But this year you went to New Hampshire. You have seen Atlanta and Memphis. You have seen men begin to talk more about issues and less about each other. You have read the report of a presidential commission which was candid, and which you could believe.

But although there is hope, nothing is yet certain. The President now talks of peace, but the war and the draft go on. Commitments have been renewed, but a man, and perhaps a movement, lie dead in Atlanta. And in our cities it is almost summer again.

So I think you had better keep moving. I think you had better demand more than what you have gotten so far until America comes home again.

THE URBAN-GRANT UNIVERSITY[3]

Clark Kerr[4]

Few men in America have been more closely associated with the new student movement than Clark Kerr, former president of the University of California at Berkeley, and currently the Chairman of the Carnegie Foundation Commission on the Future of Higher Education. Similarly, his understanding of the workings of the "multiversity" is matched by few.

Of the youth of the land, with whom his relationship has been extensive and at times vigorously tense, he has written a good deal. He admits that the new generation has many facets, and that easy generalizations about it are not likely to be persuasively telling. However, he believes that "exaggeration is one word that fits this new generation." Writing in the New York *Times Magazine* in mid-1967, he remarked: "It has exaggerated itself. It has been exaggerated by the news media. It has been exaggerated and also used, for their own purposes, by the left and the right. And, as a result, seldom in history have so many people feared so much for so little reason from so few." In this sense, youth "reflects its society," he said in an address at the University of Puerto Rico on March 25, 1967, "but often in an exaggerated fashion. It magnifies and to some extent distorts the current characteristics of its society." On the other hand, it "may, also, at times be more sensitive to new developments." And this, says Mr. Kerr, "makes the study of youth an especially rewarding one, for through youth some aspects of the nature of a society can be understood more fully and more quickly. . . ."

Just as the new generation has many facets, so must the educational experience be multisided to meet the needs of a swiftly changing society. A widely heralded proposal to join the college and the city was voiced by Mr. Kerr on October 18, 1967. Speaking at the Centennial Meeting of the City College Chapter of Phi Beta Kappa in New York City, he suggested that "we need a new

[3] Centennial Meeting of the City College (Gamma) Chapter of Phi Beta Kappa, New York City, October 18, 1967. Text furnished by Mr. Kerr and Mr. I. E. Levine, Director of Public Relations of The City College. Permission to reprint granted by Mr. Kerr and Mr. Benjamin J. Klebaner, president, Gamma Chapter, Phi Beta Kappa.

[4] For biographical note, see Appendix.

model to add to our existing models for universities in the United States." Just as the land-grant-college movement, initiated about a hundred years ago, came to the assistance of agriculture in America, so the urban-grant university must now come to the service of the beleaguered cities. This is an extension of the familiar doctrine of public service. The colleges and universities—as well as a variety of other institutions, private and public—are charged with a new mission. They must help to restore our cities, aid in the elimination of poverty, provide young people with skills for satisfying and gainful employment, and come importantly to the aid of the disadvantaged. In Mr. Kerr's words, the nation needs "sixty-seven urban-grant universities to stand beside its sixty-seven land-grant universities."

"The urban-grant university," said Mr. Kerr, "should be concerned with the urban environment in its totality, its architecture, its space use, its cultural programs and recreational facilities." While the city should get the main emphasis in this new university, it should also "follow the land-grant model in its concerns for all the mainstreams of intellectual thought and discovery." Mr. Kerr "launched a trial balloon," wrote Fred M. Hechinger, Education Editor of the New York *Times*, "for a program offering a radical cure of the country's worst domestic disease—the city slums." Continued Mr. Hechinger, "The land-grant colleges became the tooling-up device for the agricultural and industrial revolution. Their agricultural agents transformed American farming." Mr. Kerr's proposal foreshadows an analogously imperative revolution for the cities. It poses the kind of challenge which prompted President Kenneth Phillips, speaking at Metropolitan State College at Denver, to say that this newly established, urban-oriented institution gave educators "a contract with humanity."

May I express to all of you my deep appreciation for the honor which you have given me. I shall cherish it because I have such boundless admiration for City College. It is a very great pleasure to participate in this centennial meeting of the City College Chapter of Phi Beta Kappa, and especially under the chairmanship of Fred Hechinger, who is one of the best-informed and wisest commentators on all types and levels of education in the United States. In this role, he performs an inestimable service to education, and all of us throughout the nation who are concerned with education greatly appreciate his work.

It has also been wonderful this evening to have a chance to visit with President Gallagher. Here, you look upon him as a New Yorker. I look upon him as a fellow Californian. He taught at the Pacific School of Religion in Berkeley, ran for Congress in the East Bay district, and, for a time, he and I held the two hottest spots in higher education in California —perhaps in the United States. We suffered together under attacks from the left and the right. But he exhibited his superior wisdom by leaving the California scene to return to this trouble-free and quiescent sanctuary known as City College. I told him this evening that I regretted his leaving California for several reasons: his friendship, the great leadership he would have given the state colleges, and also because his departure left only one lightning rod remaining, and there was a lot of lightning.

For a good many years I have watched City College from afar. I've known many of your graduates as graduate students at the University of California, and many also as faculty members. I sometimes thought that if the City College alumni were to leave the University of California, certain departments would disappear entirely. I am, of course, quite conscious of the fact that one out of every twenty-five Ph.D.'s in the United States is a graduate of City College or one of her sister institutions in the City University. I know that City College shares with the Berkeley campus of the University of California and the University of Illinois the distinction of being the leading source of undergraduates who go on to receive doctoral degrees. I am also aware that City College has stood with the University of Chicago and the Berkeley campus as one of the three historic centers of political activism by students. It is interesting to speculate on what these three campuses have in common, why for so many years they have been centers for so much activity. To begin with, of course, each one is a key institution in a key metropolitan area of the nation. Each is relatively large and, beyond that, of high quality. So one may speak of City College as the Berkeley of the East or Berkeley as the City College of the West. All three have had their share of student unrest, and none has found any final solution to these problems. All of us, however, have discovered some things that won't work, and, if I may make a reference to an incident at City College during the thirties—for those of you of that vintage—we have learned that the problems of students cannot be handled by poking an umbrella at them.

I have also known City College as a very stern competitor for faculty talent, as the College became more famous and as you raised your salaries to higher and higher levels, making them increasingly competitive with the University of California. And, of course, City College is the first and most famous of the municipally-supported tuition-free colleges in the United States.

A centennial meeting is a time to look back and also to look ahead, and I should like to make a few comments in both directions. A hundred years ago, in 1867, City College was emerging from the Civil War years. It had just changed its name from the Free Academy. It was a fairly traditional liberal arts college, with clubs and fraternities and sports being extremely important in college life. But there were two events taking place which helped set some of the distinctive characteristics of City College for the ensuing century. A hundred years ago, there was established here a Phi Beta Kappa chapter, the second in New York and the sixteenth in the nation. And there was also established the first freely-elected student government in the United States. These two events cast their shadow across the future, as City College raised the intellectual stature of students and faculty, and also became a center for student participation in all sorts of activities. Over this hundred years, City College has grown with the city and changed with the city. It will continue to grow, and I am sure it will continue to change.

Now I should like to turn to the future, and I have chosen to talk this evening about the urban-grant university —a new university model, its new assignments and the intensified controversies which may surround it.

The land-grant university movement, as you know, is a little more than a hundred years old. A key purpose of the land-grant movement was to help agriculture throughout the United States. Today these land-grant institutions have risen to great heights of service to much of society. They presently number 67 out of some 2,300 colleges and universities in the nation, but they turn out one third of all the Ph.D. degrees. In some fields the rate is much higher: 100 per cent in agriculture, for example, and 50 per cent in the biological sciences, 50 per cent in engineering, and 50 per cent in the health professions. Showing their heritage to this very day, they turn out a far smaller proportion of advanced degrees in areas like philosophy and law, foreign languages and the other humanities.

The land-grant idea was one of the great ideas in the history of the United States and of higher education throughout the world. These institutions have contributed enormously to American agriculture and technology, making both the most productive in the world. And they have made great contributions to their particular regions as well as to the nation. How did they accomplish this? They did it, to a large extent, by turning their backs on the then-established model of a college. To the traditional classical curriculum, they added research on the problems of agriculture, and then extension directly to the farm, to help the individual farmer. But beyond the research and beyond the extension work, there was in many of these land-grant institutions a spirit—a spirit of concern, of responsibility and of service—which was really quite remarkable.

Tonight I should like to suggest that we need a new model to add to our existing models for universities in the United States. I have called this new model the urban-grant university. I have specifically not spoken of the urban university. The term *urban university* is used in some very strange ways. It is used for universities that receive some financial support from the city. It is also used for any university located in an urban setting, however uncomfortable that institution may be in its setting, however much it may wish it were located someplace else, and however much its concern with the urban community may be limited to combating the urban blight in its immediate neighborhood. Many institutions around the country called urban universities have turned their backs on their own cities.

I use the term *urban-grant,* instead, to indicate a type of university which would have an aggressive approach to the problems of the city, where the city itself and its problems would become the animating focus, as agriculture once was and to some extent still is of the land-grant university. Specifically, I should like to propose that we create, to stand beside the sixty-seven land-grant universities, some sixty-seven urban-grant universities, at least one for each city of over a quarter of a million and several for the very large cities. Not all of these would have to be new institutions, although I hope some would be new. Some institutions could be reoriented; some institutions could have their involvement with urban affairs intensified. A great many new colleges and universities are going to be created in the United States by the end of this century. President Johnson has suggested that, over the next decade, a hundred new colleges and universities may be started each year. My own guess is that there may be more nearly fifty. My proposal is that some of these new institutions each year be of the urban-grant type, to be fully useful to the modern society.

I use the term *urban-grant* to imply something beyond location and orientation, namely, that the Federal Government should aid the urban-grant university as it has the land-grant university. The Federal Government might help make the land available as part of urban renewal. Perhaps as new urban transportation systems are developed with Federal support, some urban-grant universities could be located at the great central stations of such systems, rising above them and thus easily accessible to all the people in the surrounding community. Or the urban-grant university might be part of the new educational park concept. We talk these days of educational parks, serving large areas of a city, to meet problems of *de facto* segregation and to allow other improvements in our grammar schools and high schools. Perhaps at the center of such an educational park should be a university.

Obviously, there are problems of finding the necessary land for central urban locations. But there are usually areas where land can be made available and where the construction of a new campus will serve to raise the level of activity of the whole surrounding neighborhood. In California, for example, I had proposals before our Board of Regents suggesting new university campuses in central San Francisco and in downtown Los Angeles. Our studies indicated that efficiently designed high-rise buildings can accommodate a large enrollment on perhaps as little as thirty-five acres.

The suggestion that the Federal Government should help with the land and with the money to build these new campuses or to change existing campuses is altogether reasonable. When the land-grant movement began, over 50 per cent of the people in the United States lived on the land; today, only 10 per cent do. The reasons for an urban-grant university now are at least as compelling as were those for the land-grant university in 1862. If you look at the history of Federal aid to education in the United States, you see that it has been responsive to the great problems of the nation. The land-grant movement, initiated by the Federal Government, was responsive to agrarian demands and to problems of national economic expansion. Then, during the depression, the Federal Government through the NYA [National Youth Administration] aided some students who otherwise could not have afforded to attend college. During World War II, in response to the nation's needs for science, the Federal Government stepped in with support for scientific research —support which has continued to the present time. The Government also provided aid to the returning GI's, and thus launched the tremendous recent expansion of the American college and university system. After Sputnik came the National Defense Education Act, and then, as people became more concerned with community health problems, tremendous sums of Federal money for the medical schools and for health research.

Today, great national problems have to do with the cities, with equality of opportunity, with the ending of poverty, with the quality of life, and I think that the Federal Government might logically respond to these problems by again aiding the proper activities of higher education. The urban-grant university might parallel the land-grant institution not only via city-oriented curricula and on-campus research studies but also by setting up experiment stations to work on the problems of the city as they once worked on the problems of the land, and by setting up intensified urban extension services like agricultural extension. As a counterpart to the county agent, I can visualize a school agent, for example—one who through the research at his university is informed about the best new techniques for language teaching and who can take this knowledge directly into the public schools in his particular city area. It is true that many urban problems are more complex than those of the land, but this very complexity makes the prospect of confronting them more important and more challenging.

There is one point where I would suggest that the urban-grant university specifically depart from the land-grant model. Rather than a system of selection of institutions by the state governments, I would much prefer to see a system of direct institutional applications to and grants from the Federal Government. These applications could be submitted by public or private institutions, by existing rural or suburban colleges willing to launch new urban campuses or new activities relating to urban problems, by existing urban colleges for expansion and reorientation of their programs, or by public agencies or private groups proposing to establish entirely new institutions. In this way the private "prestige" institutions of the country could participate along with leading state universities and other types of colleges. The grants would be awarded on the basis of merit and initiative, rather than merely by automatic geographical distribution among the states. The participation of some prestige institutions, both public and private, I believe to be highly important to the initial success of the urban-grant movement.

American colleges and universities now face some urgent new assignments. One is to draw in those people who aren't with us today—to their loss and to ours as well. Townsend Harris, the father of City College, of the Free Academy, set forth this destiny for City College:

> To open the doors to all. Let the children of the rich and the poor take their seats together and know of no distinction save that of industry, good conduct and intellect.

And this destiny has been fulfilled—up to a point—by City College. From the very beginning, it has extended equality of opportunity through education to new groups of people, particularly the children of immigrants, just as the land-grant institutions extended educational opportunities to the children of farmers and workers.

But access to college is not sufficiently broad today. We have what Gunnar Myrdal calls an "underclass," and we are not drawing out from this underclass the ability that is there. A start has been made, but we must do far more. Without intending to neglect the problems of other groups, let me note that only half as many Negroes go to a college or university today as is true of the rest of the population, and half of that one half go to completely segregated Negro colleges and universities. We have an enormous task of opening the doors to all and of bringing in those groups that have not yet been made full members of American society. And I think this is a key responsibility of the urban-grant university.

Whenever a new college or university campus is established—at least we found this to be the case in California—the number of people going on to a college or university from that area is increased, even though not all may attend the new local institution. The mere existence of a campus close by seems to raise the aspirations of the people surrounding it. Moving directly into the areas of deprivation, as the University of Illinois has done with its Chicago Circle campus, hopefully will bring new people into the colleges and universities.

Every effort should be made, of course, to draw in students from outside the immediate community as well, so that the urban-grant university does not become as segregated as its suburban or rural counterparts. The drawing power will depend in part on the general excellence of the institution. Beyond that, however, I believe there are many students today from all walks of life who are eager to participate in new approaches to our social problems and who would find the urban-grant university an attractive and stimulating setting for their college work.

Beyond drawing in new groups and making their talents available more fully to the nation, the urban-grant university will find many city problems that need to be attacked more directly. In recent years there has been much talk but little effective action. In fact, I think I could make a case that some universities and colleges of the nation are less involved in municipal problems today than they were a third of a century ago. The University of Chicago is less involved than it was in the thirties when Paul Douglas and Charles Merriam were active. And this is true of many other places as well. Rather than moving toward the problems of our cities, we've been moving away from them. There is, for example, an Association of Urban Universities which dates back to 1914 and has 100 members, including Harvard. It is only recently, however, that Harvard has paid attention to the blight of sections of Cambridge or to urban problems more generally. Many of these universities have been *in* the urban setting, but they have not been *of* it.

May I say that I went back and looked over the City College Centennial addresses of 1947. What were they on? Looking to a new century of service, they spoke of the new science, the new international order, liberalizing the liberal arts college, the problems of organized labor and of the business college. There was no mention of the ghetto. There was no mention of equality of opportunity. There was no mention of urban blight. There was no mention of the inadequacies of the school system at the primary and secondary levels. But these are precisely what the concerns of the urban-grant university, I think, should be. It should come in with its shirt sleeves rolled up.

I think it should take some responsibility for the over-all school system of its city. I recently attended a conference in Williamsburg on "The World Crisis in Education"—it is really the world *crises* in education. There was a very persuasive point made, in a section called "The Democratization of Education," that those systems which were the most democratized, in the sense that access was based most on merit, were in those nations whose universities had a major responsibility for the entire educational system, including the high schools and the elementary schools. Not only the urban-grant universities but universities generally ought to be looking back more to the high schools. There has been improvement in science- and mathematics-teaching, for example, because of the interest of the universities. But, by and large, the universities have taken what has come to them and have not really tried to give full assistance to the high schools and their very difficult problems. The universities could assist in a number of ways, helping to improve the quality of the curriculum and the text books, helping to identify people of great potential who, because of their home life or their cultural background, have not seriously considered the prospect of higher education. My experience in California was that the high schools were eager for more contact and assistance than the universities generally were willing to give to them. Of course, this has to be a two-way street. The high schools and the grammar schools can say something about the university and what it does, too, because university curricula and requirements have an impact all along the line on the operation of the earlier schools. The urban-grant university could help provide the framework for this interaction with the city's public school system.

I think, also, the urban-grant university should take some responsibility for the health services of the area. I think that the medical school of the future, if it does its job properly, will be more involved with the health of the surrounding community than the land-grant university was ever involved with the farmers of its state. It will be concerned not just with its university hospital, but with the quality of other hospitals and the development of health centers.

The urban-grant university should be concerned with the urban environment in its totality, its architecture, its space use, its cultural programs and recreational facilities.

Let me add emphatically, however, that the city should not be the sole concern of the urban-grant university. Certainly that should be a central emphasis, but the urban-grant university should from the first plan to follow the land-grant model in its concerns for all the mainstreams of intellectual thought and discovery.

There are a few existing colleges and universities in the United States today that approach in some respects the urban-grant institution I have sketched, but I know of none which could be held up as a full model. The land-grant university turned away from the model of the classical university and eventually had a profound impact on that type of university, so that the Harvard of today is more a land-grant institution—without the land—than the classical university it once was. And so, I believe, the urban-grant university can enter the American scene as a new model, eventually affecting all the others. And some universities will rise to heights of distinction on the urban-grant model, as have many on the land-grant approach.

This new type of university will inevitably find itself embroiled in controversy. There will be a controversy within it over the question of quality. A former president of the University of Minnesota once said that the state universities hold that there is no intellectual service too undignified for them to perform. I disagree with that. But I also disagree with the idea that because something is a city problem, it is not worthy of high-quality attention. I have seen faculty members who would work on an international problem, or on a national problem, or on the problems of local government in some other country, but not on the problems of their own city, because they regarded such work as somehow beneath them. Granted, it can be done at a low-quality level, as can work on national and international problems. But that is not necessary. We should recognize that local city problems today need and justify work of the very highest quality.

Nor should the student body be expected to be of lower quality, even though it might be desirable to adjust admission standards somewhat to help make the urban-grant university more accessible to minority group students whose earlier educational experience may not have been completely adequate. I have a sense that faculty members across the country increasingly want to make a contribution to the problems of these students, and they feel that they can. They certainly do not intend to lower the quality of the final product that comes out of the college. Rather, by greater attention and greater concern, they intend to help make up for the deficiencies of the earlier years.

These new endeavors will also see some battles among those who want to remain secluded and aloof from immediate problems, as against those who want to work toward the solution of those problems, and as against those who believe the problems can be solved only by changing the entire system. The land-grant institutions did not face so great an internal dispute about their role. Given the nature and intensity of the problems of the cities and the nation today, however, I can easily see disagreements involving students and faculty members over whether it is better to ignore the problems or to work with them or to work against the entire system. To handle the controversy on the campus among these points of view, there will have to be some rules on how opposition is mounted, and I think this is basically the responsibility of the faculty. Surely, we want free speech. Surely, we want criticism. But it must be within the law and it must be in a form that does not interfere with the proper functions of the campus.

Beyond the internal conflicts, this kind of university will be bound to face a great deal of external conflict about what it is doing. There will be those, for example, who will view with apprehension the potential political alliance of the students and the ghetto dwellers. Others will fear the potential involvement of the university in partisan urban politics. The already existing urban institutions, which are for the most part not doing the job of the urban-grant university as I visualize it, will nevertheless view any new institution or new activity as a competitor.

The land-grant institution encountered some external opposition, but not really very much. There were occasional disputes over findings about the relative merits of oleomargarine and butter. I recall a case I had in California, where one of our professors made a study which got headlines, concluding that whiskey not only tasted better than milk but was better for you, and that the older you got, the better it was, until at a certain age milk was an absolute evil and whiskey an immense benefit. I heard a good deal about these findings from the dairy interests and the allied agricultural interests. And there are always some problems from the external community when a faculty member says, for example, that farm wages ought to be higher. But the early land-grant institution faced essentially in one direction, toward the farmers, and served them, and naturally found little criticism there—except that there be more service and that it be more practical.

The urban-grant university, dealing with the problems of the city, will have to face in many directions, not one. When you deal with urban problems, you deal with urban controversies and with urban politics. And so, for this university to work effectively, there will have to be a considerable amount of public understanding—especially understanding of the distinction between service based on applications of knowledge and positions taken because of partisan politics. Beyond that, the institution will need an excellent system of buffers, and this is particularly a challenge to the trustees. I think that they should be selected on a nonpolitical basis and carefully screened, and that they should appreciate that their job is to protect the institution rather than to intensify the pressures from the external community.

There are strong indications today of a widening gulf between our universities, whatever their setting and orientation, and the general public. Some view the universities as elitist institutions apart from the everyday problems of the community. Many resent the criticisms of society that originate on university campuses. Others see the universities as sources of new ideas that are changing people's lives in ways they fear or don't understand or approve. What we need is more contact, not less, between the people and the universities. We must bridge the gulf between the intellectual community and the surrounding society because, if that gulf is permitted to widen, the intellectual community cannot get the resources and support to make it effective and the people cannot be served by intellect. The urban-grant university can provide such a bridge and, if the greater participation will result in greater controversy, we must be prepared to accept it and deal with it.

And so I would like to urge that we consider the urban-grant university as a positive approach to some of the greatest of our national problems. During World War II we turned to our universities for a vital contribution to national survival. Cannot the intellectual resources that created the new age of science now tackle the equally explosive problem of our cities? The threat is as real and the obligation surely as great.

The university can come increasingly to aid the renovation of our cities, and in return the university can be inspired by the opportunities and strengthened by the participation.

If we make this new step forward, if we aggressively accept the challenge of the problems of the great city, if we desire to participate intimately in their solution and to make knowledge serve to the full extent it can, then and only then will higher education in the United States have risen to the challenge of the times.

IN BEHALF OF A TROUBLED NATION[5]

John W. Gardner[6]

In a speech before a Youth Leadership meeting at Stevens Point, Wisconsin, on October 23, 1967, John W. Gardner remarked:

> We are producing the most educated, articulate and brilliant sidewalk superintendents the world has ever seen. We have a limitless supply of people with the intelligence and expertise to analyze the society's problems, but very, very few with the motivation and stamina to leap in and help solve them.

He called for a "great surge of citizen dedication to cope with the aggravated problems on the national scene, including war, inequality of opportunity, deterioration of the cities, pollution, population control, poverty, and threats to individuality." In an earlier address at Yeshiva University on June 12, 1967, Mr. Gardner had listed substantially the same urgencies as constituting the agenda for the younger generation.

A man of deep loyalty to high ideals, he is also uncommonly practical. The good or the great society will not come easily, he believes. Everyone, and especially youth, must face up to a trying assignment, one that begins with a

> long, hard apprenticeship [which] is required to accomplish change in the modern world. It's a complex world. It can't be run by the untrained or changed by the untrained. And after they're trained they have to have the fortitude and the staying power essential to the long, difficult task of accomplishing social change. Making a bad world better is tough, grinding, never-ending work. It's not for people whose chief interest is in posturing or striking an attitude or bandying words or venting the anger of youth.

Mr. Gardner has a sensitive, perceptive insight into the public and private agonies of our time. He has, moreover, an equally clear view of the nature and dimension of the commitment Americans must make if a great society is ever to be attained. Trained in

[5] University of North Carolina, Chapel Hill, October 12, 1967. Text furnished by Harold R. Levy, Special Assistant to Mr. Gardner, The Urban Coalition, with permission for this reprint.

[6] For biographical note, see Appendix.

psychology, he taught for several years at women's colleges in New England, then became associated with the Carnegie Corporation, serving as its president from 1955 to 1965. President Johnson appointed him Secretary of Health, Education, and Welfare in 1965, a post he held until his resignation in January 1968 when he became head of the Urban Coalition. This organization of leaders in local government, labor, civil rights, and professional and business groups aims to come to grips, through the efforts of local committees, with the worsening ills in the nation's cities.

The foregoing themes run through several of Mr. Gardner's speeches. They receive singularly apt expression in the address, reprinted below, which he delivered at a convocation exercise at the University of North Carolina, in Chapel Hill, on October 12, 1967. Coming after the summer disorders, it articulates his previous theses on America's crises with the threatening divisiveness of civil uprisings. "Today," he remarked, "the first duty of responsible citizens is to bind together rather than tear apart. The fissures in our society are already dangerously deep. We need greater emphasis on the values that hold us together." He called for a "shared allegiance," for "if the nation is to have any future, people have to care about the common enterprise."

A soft-spoken man with no zest for the in-fighting of practical politics, Mr. Gardner reminds us eloquently through his speeches that man's proper dedication to his country calls for resolute faith, courage and persistence, as well as a philosophic attitude which recognizes certain priorities of social values.

My present job gives me a close-up view of the domestic problems of this nation. I'd like to talk about those problems, and about the mood of the nation.

In the early years of this republic, our people had wonderfully high hopes for the new nation. It was to be a model for all mankind, a city on a hill, a haven of liberty and reason and justice.

Today we are unrivaled in wealth and power. We have all the outward trappings of success. What of the dream?

I don't think anyone would deny that we are uneasy in our affluence. Do I need to recite the list of anxieties—racial strife, poverty in the midst of plenty, urban decay, crime, and so on and on?

The Bible says, "Thou shalt grope at noonday, as the blind gropeth in darkness." One feels occasionally that for us it is that kind of noonday.

But it isn't.

There is a kind of comfort in thinking that our troubles are more distressing than ever before. But a close reading of history denies us that comfort. The truth is that our blessings are greater than ever before. Our troubles are no worse. They are different.

It was an error to suppose, as so many once supposed, that we could fashion a society free of problems. The problems will never cease. They will only change their character.

What is the character of the problems we face in this nation today? How shall we cope with them?

The problems themselves are easily identified. Among them I would list the search for an enduring peace, the eradication of poverty, renewal of the cities, the requirement that we do justice to Negro Americans, the improvement of education, population control, the preservation of our natural environment, the reshaping of governmental processes, and economic growth.

But we could discuss those items exhaustively without ever getting to the sources of uneasiness for many Americans today, an uneasiness that stems not from any one problem but from all, an uneasiness that goes directly to the question of where we are headed, of our health and soundness as a society, and of the relationship between the individual and society.

Ours is a vast and complex society. It's hard to know where you fit in—if indeed you do fit in. It's hard to identify anything you can call your community. It's hard to say who your leaders are—if there are any leaders in an intricately organized society. It's hard to feel any responsibility for what happens, or to feel any pride if things happen well, or to know what to do about it when they don't.

We don't want an impersonal society in which everyone is anonymous, in which no one has a sense of belonging, in which individuality is smothered by organization, in which rootlessness is the universal condition and irresponsibility the universal affliction.

But how are we to avoid those hazards?

One thing we are going to have to do is to restore a sense of community and participation at the local level, which is the only level that will have immediate meaning for large numbers of Americans.

Everything about modern life seems to conspire against a sense of community—and as a result we have lost something that most of us need very much.

We need the assurance of identity that a healthy community offers. We need the mutual obligations of community life. Above all, perhaps, we need the sense of participation— and the experience of participation—that is possible in a coherent community.

All that we know about the individual and society, and much that we know about the learning process suggest that the individual actively participating is better than the individual inert or passive—a better learner, a better citizen, a more complete person, a more self-respecting individual.

The nonparticipant individual, without roots, without a sense of identity or belonging, is a hazard to everyone including himself. He is a ready recruit to strange causes. He is always liable to lash out in desperate efforts to find meaning and purpose. We have too long pretended that people can live their lives without those ingredients. They cannot. And if they cannot find socially worthy meanings and purposes they will cast about desperately and seize upon whatever comes to hand—extremist philosophies, nihilist politics, bizarre religions, far-out protest movements.

Individuals actively participating in a community where they can see their problems face to face, know their leaders personally, sense the social structure of which they are a part —such individuals are the best possible guaranty that the intricately organized society we are heading into will not also be a dehumanized, depersonalized machine. They are also the best hope for curing the local apathy, corruption and slovenliness that make a mockery of self-government in so many localities.

Responsibility is the best of medicines. When people feel that important consequences (for themselves and others) hang on their acts, they are apt to act more wisely. It is not always easy to have that sense of responsibility toward a distant Federal Government. It helps if the ground on which responsibility is tested is at one's doorstep. Every man should be able to feel that there is a role for him in shaping his local institutions and local community.

To achieve that goal, as President Johnson has so often emphasized, we are going to have to have far greater concern for the vitality of state and local government. We shall need vigorous local leadership in and out of government. A great many of our best people are going to have to roll up their sleeves and pitch in to help make this society work.

To eradicate poverty, rebuild our central cities, lift our schools to a new level of quality and accomplish the other formidable tasks before us will require a great surge of citizen dedication. Everyone will have to lend a hand. Industry, labor, minority groups, state and local government, the universities, the churches, farm groups, the press—all will have to pitch in.

If we imagine that the Federal Government alone, or Federal, state and local governments alone can solve those problems, and that everyone else can stand by and play sidewalk superintendent, we are deceiving ourselves. It won't work. The renewal of our cities, the rebuilding of our society will require a barn-raising spirit of mutual endeavor.

If that isn't clear to you, then perhaps you haven't grasped the dimensions of the tasks facing this nation. The problems won't solve themselves, and they won't be advanced toward solution by bombast or hand wringing or cynicism or rage or self-pity on the part of any of us. They will yield only to unremitting effort by people who have the resilience of spirit and steadiness of purpose to do the work of the day as it has always been done—against odds.

We can dream great dreams and talk brilliantly of what is now bad that should be better. But when the time for doing comes—and it's long past—we must recognize that, as President Johnson put it, the kind of society we want is going to have to be built brick by brick in the heat of the day, by people who have taken the trouble to learn how the society runs and how it can be changed.

The problems are real. It doesn't require the instincts of a reformer or the eye of a muckraker to detect social evils in this land today. All it requires is the ability to follow the newspapers, to scan the data of infant mortality among the poor, to read the crime statistics, to see the manifold signs of urban disintegration, to observe the bitterness of racial conflict.

I imagine that for most of us gathered here today life is reasonably comfortable. It is easy to suppose that we are safely insulated from the problems that beset this land, that they are someone else's problems, not ours.

But they are grimly and irrevocably the problems of our generation, and none of us can escape. There isn't any place to hide. The consequences of poverty, racial conflict, environmental pollution, urban decay, and other problems will affect the quality of life for everyone here today, and for everyone in this land, the comfortable and the uncomfortable. It won't be a decent life for any of us until it is for all of us.

Consider the recent turn toward violence. Where will it lead? Where *can* it lead? There are bitter and vindictive people on both sides who hope for the worst. But you and I have to believe that a saner path is possible.

Despair in the ghettos cannot be cured by savagery in the streets. Violence begets violence. It is time to speak out against those on either side who through words or actions contribute to conflagrations of bitterness and rage. They wreak more havoc than they know. They may create ruinous cleavages and paralyzing hatreds that will make it virtually impossible for us to function as a society.

This is a day of dissent and divisiveness. Everyone speaks with unbridled anger in behalf of his point of view or his party or his people. More and more, hostility and venom are the hallmarks of any conversation on the affairs of the nation.

There used to be only a few chronically angry people in our national life. Today all seem caught up in mutual re-criminations—Negro and white, rich and poor, conservative and liberal, hawk and dove, Democrat and Republican, labor and management, North and South, young and old.

I've listened to them all, and at this moment I'd like to say a word not for or against any of them but in behalf of a troubled nation.

Today the first duty of responsible citizens is to bind together rather than tear apart. The fissures in our society are already dangerously deep. We need greater emphasis on the values that hold us together.

We need a greater common allegiance to the goals and binding values of the national community. A society or a nation is more than just a lot of people. A lot of people are a crowd or a population. To merit the term *society* or *nation* they have to have some shared attitudes and beliefs, and a shared allegiance. If the nation is to have any future, people have to care quite a lot about the common enterprise.

We know that many are willing to die for their country. We also have to care enough to live for it. Enough to live less comfortably than one might in order to serve it. Enough to work with patience and fortitude to cure its afflictions. Enough to forgo the joys of hating one another. Enough to make our most cherished common purposes prevail.

Today extremists of the right and the left work with purposeful enthusiasm to deepen our suspicion and fear of one another and to loosen the bonds that hold the society together. The trouble, of course, is that they may succeed in pulling the society apart. And will anyone really know how to put it together again?

The cohesiveness of a society, the commitment of large numbers of people to live together and work together, is a fairly mysterious thing. We don't know what makes it happen. If it breaks down we don't know how one might go about repairing it.

Back of every great civilization, behind all the panoply of power and wealth is something as powerful as it is insubstantial, a set of ideas, attitudes and convictions—and the confidence that those ideas and convictions are viable.

No nation can achieve greatness unless it believes in something—and unless that something has the moral dimensions to sustain a great civilization.

If the light of belief flickers out, then all the productive capacity and all the know-how and all the power of the nation will be as nothing, and the darkness will gather.

If enough people doubt themselves and their society, the whole venture falls apart. We must never let anger or indignation or political partisanship blur our vision on that point.

In Guatemala and southern Mexico one can observe the Indians who are without doubt the lineal descendants of those who created the Mayan civilization. Today they are a humble people, not asking much of themselves or the world, and not getting much. A light went out.

The geography and natural resources are virtually unchanged; the genetic make-up of the people is no doubt much the same. They were once a great people. Now they do not even remember their greatness. What happened?

I suspect that in the case of the Mayans, the ruling ideas were too primitive to sustain a great civilization for long.

What about our own ideas? Can they sustain a great civilization?

The answer depends on what ideas we are talking about. Americans have valued and sought and believed in many different things—freedom, power, money, equality, justice, technology, bigness, success, comfort, speed, peace, war, discipline, freedom from discipline and so on.

I like to believe that most Americans would agree on which of those values might serve as the animating ideas for a great civilization.

In my present job, I deal with a side of American society in which the existence of certain ruling ideals is visible and inescapable. I see children being taught, the sick healed, the aged cared for, the crippled rehabilitated, the talented nurtured and developed, the mentally ill treated, the weak strengthened.

Those tasks are not done by unbelieving people. Those tasks are carried forward by people who have at heart what I like to call the American Commitment.

I believe that when we are being most true to ourselves as Americans we are seeking a society in which every young person has the opportunity to grow to his full stature; a society in which every older person can live out his years in dignity; a society in which no one is irreparably damaged by circumstances that can be prevented.

All too often we have been grievously unfaithful to those ideas. And that infidelity can be cured only by deeds. Such ideas cannot be said to be alive unless they live in the acts of men, unless they are embedded in our laws, our social institutions, our educational practices, our political habits, our ways of dealing with one another. We must act in the service of our beliefs.

Every individual is of value.

The release of human potential, the enhancement of individual dignity, the liberation of the human spirit—those are the deepest and truest goals to be conceived by the hearts and minds of the American people.

And those are ideas that can sustain and strengthen a great civilization. But we must be honest about them. We must live by them. And we must have the stamina to hold to our purposes through times of confusion and controversy.

CHANGING THE PECKING ORDER[7]

HAROLD HOWE II[8]

Some 57 million persons are enrolled in the public and private schools and colleges of the United States. Such figures point up the awesome responsibility of the teachers and administrators who direct and shape the instruction which will equip the students for fruitful participation in society. While the local communities continue to control the educational programs, Federal assistance in dealing with problems of common concern throughout the country is widely confirmed. And the historic resistance to such help has in recent years weakened materially.

By a kind of general consent we have come to view education as the magical key which opens doors to influence, power, and economic security. Moreover, we have given the symbols of educational attainment—ratings on tests, certificates, and degrees—a dignity and status which, in the opinion of some modern critics, are disproportionate to their worth, if not in fact destructive of the best democratic ideals of education. We have allowed credentials, so the argument runs, to usurp the dictates of good judgment.

This is not a stricture on degrees, per se. Rather, it is a reminder that uncritical acceptance of them as the sole passport to a job or professional assignment is arguable practice. This is largely the thesis developed by Harold Howe II in his address before the College Entrance Examination Board, meeting in Chicago on October 24, 1967. The Commissioner of Education remarked that taking the symbol for the substance

> is not the hallmark of good and careful judgment or of attention to individual differences. We should never *automatically* assume that the person with some letters after his name will perform better than the person without those letters. We should never *automatically* assume that the person who has held a job precisely like one we are trying to fill will perform better than the person who has no comparable experience.

[7] College Entrance Examination Board, Chicago, Illinois, October 24, 1967. Text furnished by Walter A. Coyne, Director of Division of Program Support, Office of Information, Department of Health, Education, and Welfare, Office of Education, with permission for this reprint.

[8] For biographical note, see Appendix.

Not a traditionalist in educational philosophy, Mr. Howe decries the use of efficiency as the sole criterion in determining whether applicants for positions meet prescribed standards. "No matter what system we use to evaluate people, we need to build in provisions for unique individuals and reasonable allowance for not-so-unique individuals who have some special attribute." What he calls the "credentialing myopia" applies both to the disadvantaged and the ones with resources and accomplishments at the highest levels. His concern is that

this credential-laden rat race doesn't permit society to establish meaningful criteria and standards that apply to the population as a whole. Nor does it allow adequately for exceptions.

A society that prides itself on equality of opportunity must somehow learn to accommodate those children who are least likely to collect adequate credentials but who may have the unrealized potential to succeed in demanding tasks.

Mr. Howe looks with favor upon the admission by some institutions of so-called "high-risk" students, and he calls for "special support services" which will provide compensatory training for those heretofore deprived of a fair opportunity. "If a student comes from a deprived background, the college has to read that into his record and learn to identify his talent and ability even though his test scores do not show it in conventional ways."

Mr. Howe was appointed to his present position by President Johnson in late 1965. Prior to accepting the post, he had taught in public and private schools, chiefly in the East. For two years he served as Executive Director of the Learning Institute of North Carolina, an organization concerned with the development of new programs for disadvantaged youngsters.

Since coming to the Office of Education, Mr. Howe has delivered a good many speeches which have attracted wide public attention. Among them was "A New Luster for College Teaching" before the American Council on Education, New Orleans, October 14, 1966, in which he decried the utilitarian aspect in the teaching of the liberal arts: "The life of the mind takes on the nature of social insurance; it becomes a kind of intellectual mouthwash to protect you from offending, by making sure that you will not prefer a minor poet to a major, or admire either for the wrong reasons." The basic shortcoming in current teaching, he declared, is "the failure to probe for the intellectual curiosity in every student and guide it in those directions which we have found over the centuries as being most important to a civilized and fulfilling life." In "The Heat in Our Kitchen," given before the School Administrators Conference in New York City, June 18, 1967, he called upon school officials "to form a third front for racial equality in the United States." And in "The Strength of a Sparrow," delivered before the Urban Schools Conference in Washington, D.C., on September 22, 1967, he dealt largely with the economic difficulties faced by the city school systems, and the consequent sharpening of cleavages between the culturally deprived children in the central city school and the more affluent children in the suburbs.

Mr. Howe's speeches are written in clear, simple language. Their lucidity brings his forthrightness on the social dilemmas of our time into sharp focus. Moreover, he invariably uses introductory material which has considerable human interest appeal. Many of the introductions to the public speeches of our time are a bit conventional, even pedestrian. Not so, ordinarily, with Mr. Howe's. And it is not uncommon for him to use the device of linking the conclusion with the introduction—that is, returning to the point of the opening story or incident when he pulls the threads of his discourse together in final summation.

It is very pleasant for me to realize that this evening I have the members of the College Entrance Examination Board temporarily at my mercy. I know that this heady monopoly won't last long, but as a former vice chairman and a long time committee member I hope you will forgive me for enjoying the opportunity to speak to you at some length, on a subject of my own choosing, without fear of interruption.

I do this, of course, by virtue of my present office. Though I am no more learned and not any wiser than I was as a member of this group, being Commissioner of Education does give me a certain leverage I didn't have before.

It is this leverage—or, more precisely, such criteria for leverage—that I mean to criticize this evening.

The barnyard hierarchy which chickens establish among themselves is a natural phenomenon that we all take for granted. We call it "the pecking order." It brings the larger, the stronger, or the more confident chickens to the feeding trough before the skinny, introverted ones, who most need to be fed. But in the hierarchy of social and occupational dominance, prestige and authority based on academic or titular credentials are human phenomena that I am afraid we cannot afford to take for granted. It is our some- what artificial human pecking order that requires some examination.

It seems to me extremely important to the survival and the health of America that we find ways for the institutions which control opportunity in our society to do so with a concern for those people who have been denied opportunity by the shortcomings of the society.

It is of desperate importance in a viable and open social system that we learn to cherish and nurture a variety of talents with adequate appreciation for each. Secretary of Health, Education, and Welfare John Gardner pinpointed this neatly for us when he wrote:

> An excellent plumber is infinitely more admirable than an incompetent philosopher. The society which scorns excellence in plumbing because plumbing is a humble activity and tolerates shoddiness in philosophy because it is an exalted activity will have neither good plumbing nor good philosophy. Neither its pipes nor its theories will hold water.

I'd like to go a step further and suggest that it is not inconceivable that our excellent plumber might also have the makings of an admirable philosopher. We have no ac- curate way of knowing that he would not. If we think he would not (and we probably do), it is most likely because he has no degree in philosophy.

Which may be a bit like saying that Socrates wasn't a good teacher because he had no teaching credential—and suggests that we have forgotten that Spinoza earned his living as a lens grinder and that Tom Edison quit school at the age of nine.

My point is that an academic degree or a diploma is a fairly good indicator of ability—but only in a negative sense; in the sense that a person who has such a degree or diploma is probably not intellectually *in*adequate.

But taking the symbol for the substance is not the hall-mark of good and careful judgment or of attention to in-dividual differences. We should never *automatically* assume that the person with some letters after his name will perform better than the person without those letters. We should never *automatically* assume that the person who has held a job precisely like one we are trying to fill will perform better than the person who has no comparable experience.

Unfortunately, people are individuals, and institutions deal in multitudes. There is never time to inspect each person, to grade him like a cut of beef, and stamp him prime, choice, or good. Administrative necessity dictates the establishment of some criteria on which to base selection.

There is considerable evidence that public policy and institutional practice make it extremely difficult for com-petent but uncredentialed persons to have a fair crack at competitive situations, whether they be social, vocational, or educational.

Without question we need broad minimum standards in a whole basketful of categories. And we need efficient ways to determine whether or not our applicants meet those stan-dards. But efficiency cannot be our only criterion. No matter what system we use to evaluate people, we need to build in provisions for unique individuals and reasonable allowance for not-so-unique individuals who have some special attribute.

I don't think we are terribly good at this.

At almost every level, in almost all fields, we find an automatic emphasis on credentials, a routine rigidity, whether the credential under consideration is a high school diploma, a Ph.D. or a certificate from a beauty college.

Before I cast any further stones (and I intend to do so), I'd like to make it clear that the Federal Government is hardly blameless in this area. This Administration, under strong directive from President Johnson, has largely elimi-nated job discrimination against women and against minority groups. But other categories of discrimination still exist.

Let me quote from a study of equal employment opportunities within my shop, the Office of Education:

> Over-all, racial discrimination is not an important problem in the Office, certainly much less prevalent than in other institutions of society, but substantial attention could be given to . . . the credential of a college degree which is evidently more important for advancement in OE than competence itself.

Elsewhere the report is more specific:

> The chance of a noncollege person being promoted across the grade nine-ten barrier (this refers to Civil Service categories nine and ten) is negligible, while the possibility of a college person being promoted across the barrier in a reasonable number of years (say three) is very high. OE policy appears to say that virtually no one without a college degree is capable of handling work above Civil Service grade nine.

The most heartening element of this report is the absence of racial discrimination per se within the Office—but I'm not sure our overdependence on sheepskin and degrees is not, in its own way, an inadvertent racial discrimination.

Professor S. M. Miller of New York University made this point last year in a paper called "Credentialism and the Education System." Pointing out that education once served as a means of ascendancy for the poor, he said it is now

> becoming a bar to the new poor's effort to change conditions. Today the insistence on education as a prerequisite for jobs is becoming a barrier to the occupational ascendancy of today's disprivileged.
>
> We have become a credential society, where one's educational level is more important than what he can do. People cannot obtain jobs that they could well fill because they lack educational qualifications. Negroes who dropped out of the educational steeplechase before getting a high school diploma cannot get jobs. Employers and the better-off do not feel that there is discrimination; rather the low-educated are "not qualified."

This credentialing myopia is by no means confined to the disadvantaged. In almost every occupation, at almost every level, one finds certification requirements of one kind or another locking people out of situations in which they might well be substantial contributors. This remains true, though we know that new technology changes job functions so fast that adaptability may be more essential in a prospective employee than any specific knowledge or specific training.

Classified ad columns are full of jobs for deliverymen, parking attendants, elevator operators, etc.—who need not have experience as long as they have high school diplomas. Though a high school education may not contribute much to the skill of an elevator operator, it does simplify the task of a personnel manager who knows that his applicants are likely to be conformists, if nothing more.

The official directory of the City of New York has forty-seven pages of very small type that list licenses, permits, or certification requirements for such diverse occupations as midwifery, ophthalmic dispensary traineeships, undertakers, oil-burner operators, and funeral directors' apprentices.

A recent letter to members of a private university club in New York City announced the appointment of a man whom I shall fictitiously call Charles Chan as general manager. It identified him as Charles Chan, CCM. What is CCM? Certified Club Manager.

I don't mean to suggest that I am against letters after people's names, nor am I against any sort of effort to insure competence or adequate skills on the part of midwives or undertakers.

What does concern me is that the route into an increasing number of occupations is a specific educational route and, for some professions, that route begins close to infancy and makes no provision for detours.

Author John Keats has written of the ferocious competition for entrance to private nursery schools. In New York City, such preschools report over 150 applications for every vacancy. This kind of competition stems from concern of the parents for their children's entrance into elementary and preparatory school (which is easier for a graduate of a "good" nursery school), and aims ultimately, of course, at entrance into a "good" college. Anxious parents have been known to hire tutors to coach three-year-olds on the Stanford Binet test and to change their religious affiliation to secure placement in desirable church-sponsored schools.

Again, I'm not against private nursery schools nor against parents who want the best education for their children. My concern is that this credential-laden rat race doesn't permit society to establish meaningful criteria and standards that apply to the population as a whole. Nor does it allow adequately for exceptions.

A society that prides itself on equality of opportunity must somehow learn to accommodate those children who are least likely to collect adequate credentials but who may have the unrealized potential to succeed in demanding tasks.

There are many bright children in inner-city schools. I think that there is a reasonable doubt that they get a fair shake. It may well be, as Marshall McLuhan has said, that it is the bright kids who drop out because school "is not where the action is." Certainly bright people drop out of college and graduate schools. But typically our schools and colleges have acted as selection agents on an economic basis (and therefore on a racial basis) rather than as purveyors of equal opportunity.

In the last few years we have established a new doctrine for elementary and secondary education; its premise is that equal educational opportunity does not result from treating all pupils equally.

The underlying basis for the Elementary and Secondary Education Act of 1965 is the conviction that our schools must do more for those pupils who come to school with less —and this includes, but is not limited to, spending more per pupil for their education.

Now it is time to ask what the colleges have done (and what they propose to do) in order to reflect this new philosophy in higher education; how they plan to give students the educational opportunities that will help them progress, and when they will forgo their role as sorting out institutions serving the "haves" and ignoring the "have-nots."

We have to remember that the high school student who sticks it out because he knows he can earn almost twice as much as his dropout friend (even if his friend is brighter) isn't *always* more valuable to society than the dropout. The student who stays in college knowing that he will probably earn $150,000 more than his friend who drops out is not *necessarily* an inquiring intellect. The graduate student writing his thesis on the Subliminal Use of Visual Symbols in 14th and 15th Century Prose and Poetry may not be on an educational quest of much significance even though it will gain him a credential. He may be, as suggested by Kingsley Amis, engaging in the Teutonic academic tradition of "casting pseudo light on nonproblems."

The promising law student who elects a law school that confers a Doctor of Jurisprudence instead of Harvard, which confers a Bachelor of Laws, is probably a realist. He knows that the J.D. can make him an instant assistant professor if he chooses to teach after graduation. With an LL.B., even from Harvard, he will probably only be offered an instructorship, although the course work and skills required for the LL.B. may be more demanding.

Until we learn how to tell when people are competent, we will continue to have a great many people going to school for the wrong reasons and a great many more who are not going to school for the wrong reasons. As managers and as admissions officers we are going to lose a lot of "mute, inglorious Miltons" unless we find some better ways to measure potential ability and unless we can serve larger numbers of people with an education which helps the individual reach the credential rather than failing him because he cannot reach it in the same fashion as others.

I don't know what the answer is; perhaps if we could confer Ph.D.'s along with citizenship and a social security number at birth, our schools would change from credentialing agencies to incubators of culture and centers of intellectual ferment. Barring such a development, we need, at the very least, to find new ways to credential people who missed their footing on some step of the social, economic, and educational escalator.

There is a paradox here: we've committed ourselves to the credentialing system, and now we need to find ways to beat it. The institutions which are involved in it must now learn to act on behalf of the people who are affected by it. Some institutions are already beginning to take an interest in high-risk students, and the Federal Government is helping support their efforts through Upward Bound, Talent Search, and a number of other compensatory programs.

But institutional efforts must go beyond taking these less credentialed youngsters into their hallowed halls; the institutions will have to offer them special support services after they get there—we can't just get rid of them if they start to fail. If their intellectual foundations are weak, then we will have to do a rebuilding job.

This is going to demand some major adjustments on the part of institutions—not a lowering of standards but the introduction of flexibility. If a student comes from a deprived background, the college has to read that into his record and learn to identify his talent and ability even though his test scores do not show it in conventional ways.

This also means that we have to read the disadvantaged background factor into college entrance examination scores before making decisions on admission. If we consider tests as diagnostic devices, they can be used to include, rather than exclude. Thus a youngster who is far behind in math may be admitted, but required to take a special compensatory math course. Perhaps colleges should add a whole year of pre-college compensatory work to the regular curriculum offerings. We're all living longer nowadays. There is no reason that some of us can't take five years to get through college. If the added time will bring success, it's more than worth it.

Our country has a tremendous investment in this sort of rebuilding. We simply can't let a whole generation go by because we've just learned the lessons of Head Start and are waiting for last year's preschoolers to reach college age. We must get some of these people into colleges now so that we can graduate more Mexican-Americans and more Negroes now. Otherwise we are going to end up with a rigidly stratified society because the whole credentialing system serves the middle class and rejects the less fortunate.

All our carefully developed forms of exclusion might make economic (if not moral) sense if society was oversupplied with skilled manpower. At a time when we face desperate shortages in almost all professions and skilled trades, it is wasteful and dangerous.

Let's take teaching for an example. Accumulated data from elementary and secondary school districts across the nation show a shortage of over 200,000 certified teachers. What does that mean? What does it take to be a certified teacher? If we move from locality to locality, from coast to coast, we find a conflicting array of certification requirements. Do they make sense? Often they do. But let's examine an individual instance:

A woman in her late twenties, a graduate of Smith College, had taught English successfully in a French school in Paris for two years, had been an editorial assistant on *Réalités* for one year and had taught French in a private preparatory school in Pennsylvania for two years. She moved to another state and applied for a job teaching French in a suburban, public elementary school.

I don't need to tell you what happened. No job, because of lack of credentials. I probably don't need to tell you, either, that a majority of states do not require language teachers to be able to speak the language they are to teach; an unfortunately large number of language teachers cannot do so.

I am sure there is an abundance of qualified but uncredentialed (note that I resist saying the reverse—credentialed but unqualified) talent available to the elementary and secondary school classrooms of this nation. But the benefits of this talent will continue to elude us as long as we are locked into a rigid credentialing system that permits us, out of fear, laziness or irresponsibility, to abandon the exercise of judgment when we make decisions about people.

I might add that there are signs of a break-through on the credential problem. Although I know some congressmen who would not consider it a virtue, both President Kennedy and President Johnson have set an example by appointing Commissioners of Education who lacked an advanced degree. On the other side of the coin is the fact that neither of these commissioners can meet the new credentials of the American Association of School Administrators.

Those who are already established in a profession or occupation are usually responsible for maintaining its standards. When a credentialing review committee is established, somehow its members always come up with tougher entrance requirements. Rarely does anyone ever suggest making it easier to get in and the possibility of getting some good people that way.

It is human nature to want to keep our club hard to get into; logic always loses when the ego is threatened. Even public relations, the last refuge for eclectic self-educated talent (after metropolitan newspapers began requiring journalism degrees for copy boys) recently instituted tough credentialing procedures—so tough that only 17 per cent of the present members of the national society were able to pass the examination. Nonetheless, new applicants will have to do so or the national society won't accept them.

These are not frivolous matters. When we determine the educational and vocational limits of individual lives by such practices, procedures and symbols, we not only do injustice to the individual but we inflict a potential talent loss of inestimable consequence to the nation.

What can we do about it? We certainly cannot do away with credentials—they are as much a part of the contemporary scene as taxes and television (and I have mixed feelings about all three).

But we can minimize their impact of a negative kind by having the wisdom to use them wisely and flexibly. We can, as I said earlier, develop some new ways to acquire them. Several Federal programs focus on this problem. They are aimed at developing new careers for the poor, jobs that provide semiprofessional status in the fields of medicine and education. We *can* do this; we can break down the professional role so that subprofessional jobs open up. More importantly we can relate the subprofessional role to the professional so that a person can shift from one to the other with greater ease. There are plenty of teacher aides and nurses aides who would make good teachers or good nurses if we could provide special training programs for them and persuade the professional establishment to accept their ability to perform professional tasks despite the absence of some of the traditionally required credentials.

We can give more credit for experience, both in hiring people and in selecting them for educational institutions. An example: When the State University of New York opens its experimental college next year, it plans to give undergraduate credit for Peace Corps experience.

Colleges and universities might relax entrance requirements for master's degree candidates. Gifted college dropouts with ten or fifteen years subsequent experience who wish to enter a master's degree program should, perhaps, be able to get a waiver of their undergraduate degree.

We must remember that some people will learn whether or not they have the advantage of college experience; that some other people, if they have staying power, can end up with degrees that really don't mean much.

We can continue to search for better ways to evaluate people, more sophisticated ways to measure ability, skill, and potential. And finally, we can build escape clauses into all our certifying, credentialing and admissions procedures to allow individual consideration of people with special situations, unique talents, or measurable handicaps.

None of this is enough to change radically the pecking order, but if we are conscientious in our effort to look at people, not paper, and offer honest second chances educationally and professionally, we may be able to help a few skinny chickens get a little closer to the feeding trough.

DISSENT AND THE SENSE OF RESPONSIBILITY

DISSENT, DISSENSION AND THE NEWS [1]

DANIEL J. BOORSTIN [2]

"Dissent," said John W. Gardner, former Secretary of Health, Education, and Welfare, "is an element of dynamism in our system. It is good that men expect much of their institutions, and good that their aspirations for improvement are ardent." But, he promptly added, "the elements of dynamism must have stabilizing counterparts." This has been the rub. Dissent continues to be widespread over issues of domestic and foreign conduct. But it has become increasingly difficult to maintain the counterpoise between resolute commitment to a public cause and what Mr. Gardner called "an unswerving commitment to keep the public peace." At a time when the liberty to speak out and to protest is not in immediate jeopardy—as the countless demonstrations attest—the perennial enigma remains unsolved and at times menacing to public order: How can the exercise of freedom be responsibly disciplined to prevent its entering upon license?

The concept of dissent contains two major facets: definition and implication. An uncommonly acute blend of these components is found in Professor Daniel J. Boorstin's lucid address of October 18, 1967, in Chicago, Illinois, before the annual meeting of the Associated Press Managing Editors' Association. Although directed to newspapermen, the speech engaged a thesis of broad concern to all citizens. Professor Boorstin spoke of dissent as "the great problem of America today." And he distinguished between disagreement and dissent:

> Disagreement is specific and programmatic, dissent is formless and unfocused. Disagreement is concerned with policy, dissenters are concerned with identity, which usually means themselves. Disagreers ask, What about the war in Vietnam? Dissenters ask, What about me? Disagreers seek solutions to common problems, dissenters seek power for themselves.

[1] The Associated Press Managing Editors' Association, Chicago, Illinois, October 18, 1967. Copyright © 1967, Daniel J. Boorstin. Text furnished by Dr. Boorstin, with permission for this reprint.

[2] For biographical note, see Appendix.

In his concluding remarks, Professor Boorstin observed that "affirmations of differentness and feeling apart cannot hold a society together." Accordingly, he inquired whether it was possible "to produce interesting newspapers that will sell but which do not yield to the temptation to create and nourish new dissent by stirring people to feel apart in new ways." In short, can newspapers dramatize what people agree upon?

For nearly twenty-five years, Professor Boorstin has been a professor at the University of Chicago, and since 1966 the Preston and Sterling Morton Professor of History. A gifted writer, he is perhaps best known for *The Americans,* the first volume of which received the esteemed Bancroft Prize in 1959 and the second volume, the equally prestigious Francis Parkman Prize. Students of public address view his two-volume *An American Primer* as an invaluable resource for the study of American oratory. "A kind of American catechism," as he put it, the set contains about seventy-five texts of documents, letters, and speeches, ranging from the Mayflower Compact of 1620 to Lyndon B. Johnson's 1965 "Address on Voting Rights." Illuminating headnotes and so-called afterlife essays accompany each item and provide fresh insight into many orations which grace the standard anthologies of public address.

Gentlemen, it's a great pleasure and privilege to be allowed to take part in your meeting. It is especially a pleasure to come and have such a flattering introduction, the most flattering part of which was to be called a person who wrote like a newspaperman.

The historians, you know, sometimes try to return that compliment by saying that the best newspapermen write like historians but I'm not sure how many of the people present would consider that a compliment.

This afternoon I would like to talk briefly about the problems we share, we historians and newspapermen, and that we all share as Americans.

About sixty years ago Mark Twain, who was an expert on such matters, said there are only two forces that carry light to all corners of the globe, the sun in the heaven and the Associated Press. This is, of course, not the only view of your role. Another newspaperman once said it's the duty of a newspaper to comfort the afflicted and afflict the comfortable.

If there ever was a time when the light and the comfort which you can give us was needed, it's today. And I would like to focus on one problem.

It seems to me that dissent is the great problem of America today. It overshadows all others. It's a symptom, an expression, a consequence and a cause of all others.

I say dissent and not disagreement. And it is the distinction between dissent and disagreement which I really want to make. Disagreement produces debate but dissent produces dissension. Dissent, which comes from the Latin, means originally to feel apart from others.

People who disagree have an argument, but people who dissent have a quarrel. People may disagree but may both count themselves in the majority, but a person who dissents is by definition in a minority. A liberal society thrives on disagreement but is killed by dissension. Disagreement is the life blood of democracy, dissension is its cancer.

A debate is an orderly exploration of a common problem that presupposes that the debaters are worried by the same question. It brings to life new facts and new arguments which make possible a better solution. But dissension means discord. As the dictionary tells us, dissension is marked by a break in friendly relations. It is an expression not of a common concern but of hostile feelings. And this distinction is crucial.

Disagreement is specific and programmatic, dissent is formless and unfocused. Disagreement is concerned with policy, dissenters are concerned with identity, which usually means themselves. Disagreers ask, What about the war in Vietnam? Dissenters ask, What about me? Disagreers seek solutions to common problems, dissenters seek power for themselves.

The spirit of dissent stalks our land. It seeks the dignity and privilege of disagreement but it is entitled to neither. All over the country on more and more subjects we hear more and more people quarreling and fewer and fewer people debating. How has this happened? What can and should we do about it?

This is my question this afternoon. In the first place I would like to remind you of one feature of the situation which suggests it may not be as desperate as it seems. This is what I would call the law of the conspicuousness of dissent which is another way of saying there never is quite as much dissent as there seems.

I will start from an oddity of the historical record which other American historians can confirm for you.

When we try to learn, for example, about the history of religion in the United States we find that what is generally described as that subject is a history of religious controversies. It's very easy to learn about the Halfway Covenant problem, the Great Awakening, the Unitarian controversies, the Americanist controversies and so on. But if we want to learn about the current of daily belief of Americans in the past it's very difficult.

And this is the parable of the problem of history. If we want to learn about the history of divorce there are many excellent histories of divorce, but if we want to learn about the history of marriage we'll find there are practically none.

Similarly if we want to learn about eating and drinking habits there are some excellent histories of vegetarianism and food fads, some first-rate histories of prohibition but almost no good histories of eating and drinking.

Why is this the case?

It is simply because of what I would call the law of the conspicuousness of dissent. Controversies, quarrels, disagreements leave a historical debris of printed matter, not to mention broken heads and broken reputations. Carry Nation smashing up a bar makes much more interesting reading and is more likely to enter the record than the peaceable activity of the bartender mixing drinks. But this may lead us to a perverse emphasis. How have people lived and thought and felt and eaten and drunk and married in the past? Interests are focused on the cataracts, the eddies, the waterfalls and whirlpools. But what of the stream?

This is a natural bias of the record and it equally affects the reporting of news. It is obvious that a sermon is less newsworthy than a debate and a debate still less newsworthy than a riot. This is all obvious but it has serious consequences for the condition of our country today. The natural bias of the record tends to lead us to emphasize and inevitably over-emphasize the extent of dissent.

Secondly, the rise and multiplication of media. The profession which you gentlemen represent together with the American standard of living leads us also towards the exaggeration of the importance of dissent in our society. Since dissent is more dramatic and more newsworthy than agreement, media inevitably multiply and emphasize dissent. It is an easier job to make a news story of men who are fighting with one another than it is to describe their peaceful living together.

All this has been reinforced by certain obvious developments in the history of the newspaper and the other media within the last half century or so—the increasingly frequent and repetitious news reporting. The movement from the weekly newspaper to the daily newspaper to several editions a day, the rise of radio reporting of news every hour on the hour with news breaks in between, all require that there be changes to report. There are increasingly voluminous spaces both of time and of print which have to be filled.

And all these reports become more and more inescapable from the attention of the average citizen. In the bar, on the beach, in the automobile, the transistor radio reminds us of the headaches of our society. Moreover, the increasing vividness of reports also tempts us to depict objects and people in motion, changing, disputing. The opportunity to show people in motion and to show them vividly had its beginning, of course, in the rise of photography and Mathew Brady's pioneer work in the Civil War and then more recently with the growth of the motion picture and television. All this tempts us to get a dramatic shot of a policeman striking a rioter or vice versa. We now have tape recorders on the scene on which people can express their complaints about anything.

Moreover, the rise of opinion is a new category. The growth of opinion polling has led to the very concept of "opinion" as something people can learn about. There was a time when information about the world was divided into the category of fact or the category of ideas. But more recently, especially with the growth of market research in this century, people now must have opinions. They are led to believe by the publication of opinion polls that their opinion—whether it be on the subject of miniskirts or marijuana or foreign policy—is something that separates them from others. Moreover, if they have no opinion, even that now puts them in a dissenting category.

Then there is the rise of what I call secondary news. News about the news. With an increasingly sophisticated readership and more and more media we have such questions as whether a news conference will be canceled; will someone refuse to make a statement; is the fact that Jackie Kennedy denied there was a supposed engagement between her and Lord Harlech itself a kind of admission. What is really news?

Moreover, the very character of American history has accentuated our tendency to dissent. We are an immigrant society. We are made up of many different groups who came here and who felt separate from one another, who were separated not so much by doctrine or belief as by the minutiae of daily life. By language, religious practices, cuisine and even manners. Until the 1930's and 40's, the predominant aim of those who were most concerned in this country with the problem of immigration was to restrict immigration or to assimilate those immigrants who were admitted. To "Americanize the immigrant"—this was the motto of those who were most concerned with this question.

But in the last few decades we have had a movement from "assimilation" to "integration." And this is an important distinction. In about the 1930's Louis Adamic began writing and in his book *A Nation of Nations* in 1945 he began an emphasis which has been often repeated. It was no longer the right of the immigrant to be Americanized, to be assimilated, it was now the right of the immigrant to remain different. The ideal ceased to be that of fitting into the total society and instead became the right to retain your differences. Symptoms of this were such phenomena in politics as the rise of the balanced ticket, a ticket which consists of outspoken and obvious representatives of different minorities. It brought with it the assumption that the only 100 per cent American is the person who is only partly American. It led General Eisenhower to make something of his German name and his German background which had not occurred to very many of us before. It encouraged John F. Kennedy to exploit his Irish background, the notion being that one was more fully American by being partly something else.

This sense of separateness and the power of minorities developed alongside two great movements. One, in the social sciences—the growth of literature, much of which stems from universities in this area, and especially from the University of Chicago—a literature of the social sciences which came to show minorities who they were, where they were, and what their power might be.

Gunnar Myrdal's book *American Dilemma,* which was quoted by the Supreme Court integration decision of 1954, was a very good illustration of this. The rise of opinion polling also led into this. People in small groups were reminded that they had a power and a locale which they had not known before. Stokely Carmichael himself has referred to this on several occasions—that he may represent a group which is not very numerous but he knows where they are. They're in crucial places where they can exercise power.

Alongside this change in our thinking and this extension of our knowledge came a change in technology which I would call the rise of "flow technology." Minimum speed forty miles an hour. This means that while formerly, in order to do damage to other people, it was necessary for you to set things in motion—to wave your arms or wield a club—now when the economy and the technology are in motion, if you want to cause damage you need only stop and the other people do the damage. This is a parable which was illustrated in the blackout in New York, the stall-ins and sit-ins. At a time when certain students seized the administration building at a neighboring university last year all they had to do was to hold that one building. All the salary checks flowed through the IBM machines in that building and they were able to throw a monkey wrench into the machinery.

This has the effect of developing what I would call a minority veto psychology. Small groups have more power than ever before. In small numbers there is strength. This results in the quest for minority identity. Whereas formerly people used to change their names to sound more American, to try to fit into the background, now the contrary seems to be occurring.

And we find symptoms of this in the intellectual world. Perhaps that is a misnomer—I should say rather in the world of those who consider themselves or call themselves intellectuals. I find in this world today, in this country, a growing belief in the intrinsic virtue of dissent. It's worth noting that some of the greatest American champions of the right to disagree and to express disagreement—Thomas Jefferson, Oliver Wendell Holmes, Jr., William James, John Dewey and others—were also great believers in the duty of the community to be peacefully governed by the will of the majority. But more recently dissent itself has been made into a virtue. Dissent for dissent's sake. We have a whole group of magazines these days dedicated not to this or that particular program or social reform nor this or that social philosophy but simply to dissent.

Professional dissenters do not and cannot seek to assimilate their program or ideals into American culture. Their main object is to preserve their separate identity as a dissenting minority. They're not interested in the freedom of anybody else. The motto of this group might be an emendation of the old maxim of Voltaire which I'm sure you've all heard. But nowadays people would say, "I do not agree with a word you say. And I will defend to the death *my* right to say so."

Once upon a time our intellectuals competed for their claim to be spokesmen of the community. Now the time has almost arrived when the easiest way to insult an intellectual is to tell him that you or most other people *agree* with him. The way to menace him is to put him in the majority for the majority must run things and must have a program and dissent needs no program.

Dissent, then, has tended to become the conformity of our most educated classes. In many circles to be an outspoken conformist, that is, to say that the prevailing ways of the community are *not* "evil," requires more courage than to run with the dissenting pack.

The conformity of nonconformity, the conformity of dissent produces little that is fruitful in its conclusions and very little effective discussion or internal debate. For the simple reason that it does not involve anybody in attacking or defending any program. Programs, after all, are the signs of "the Establishment."

The situation that I have described leads to certain temptations which afflict the historian as well as the newsman and among these temptations I would like to include the tendency to stimulate and accentuate dissent rather than disagreement. To push disagreement toward dissent so that we can have a more dramatic or reportable event. To push the statement of a program toward the expression of a feeling of separateness or isolation.

There is an increasing tendency also to confuse disagreement with dissent. For example, the homosexuals in our society who are a group who feel separate (and are from one point of view a classic example of what we mean by the dissenter) now articulate their views in declarations and statements. Nowadays they become disagreers, they have formed

Mattachine societies, they issue programs and declarations. This, I would say, is good.

But on the other hand we find disagreers who are increasingly tempted to use the techniques of dissent. Students who disagree about the war in Vietnam use the techniques of dissent, of affirming their secession from society, and this is bad.

The expressions of disagreement may lead to better policy but dissent cannot.

The affirmations of differentness and feeling apart cannot hold a society together. In fact these tend to destroy the institutions which make fertile disagreement possible, and fertile institutions decent. A sniper's bullet is an eloquent expression of dissent, of feeling apart. It doesn't express disagreement. It is formless, inarticulate, unproductive. A society of disagreers is a free and fertile and productive society. A society of dissenters is a chaos leading only to dissension.

Now I would like in conclusion to suggest that we are led to a paradox. A paradox which must be solved. A free and literate society with a high standard of living and increasingly varied media, one that reaches more and more people more and more of the time—such a society finds it always easier to dramatize its dissent rather than disagreement. It finds it harder and harder to discover, much less to dramatize, its agreement on anything. This ends then in some questions which I will pose to you gentlemen to which I hope you may have answers. At least they seem to me to be crucial ones.

First, is it possible to produce interesting newspapers that will sell but which do not dramatize or capitalize on or catalyze dissent and dissension, the feeling of apartness in the community? Is it possible to produce interesting newspapers that will sell but which do not yield to the temptation to create and nourish new dissent by stirring people to feel apart in new ways?

Second, is it possible at the same time to find new ways of interesting people in disagreement in specific items and problems and programs and specific evils?

Finally, is it possible for our newspapers—without becoming Pollyannas or chauvinists or super patriots or Good Humor salesmen—to find new ways of expressing and affirming, dramatizing and illuminating, what people agree upon?

This is your challenge. The future of American society in no small measure depends on whether and how you answer it.

THE BETRAYAL OF IDEALISM [3]

John Sloan Dickey [4]

Convocation and commencement addresses make up a substantial part of the rhetorical fare at schools and colleges. A representative sample of the number and quality of the addresses may be checked simply by reading the ones that are reprinted in the *Congressional Record* and "Extension of Remarks" during the early fall and spring. Although students may be mildly reluctant to admit it—especially if their attendance is required or at least urgently recommended—many of the talks are uncommonly good. And, by and large, they are carefully prepared. While often labeled as the natural home of the platitude, the ceremonial talk is not really any more deserving of this charge than deliberative speaking. Many commencement and related addresses doubtless contain overworked themes; but if the themes have persistency of value, why should we think ill of them simply because they are refrains? We do not ordinarily have the same suspicion of repeated arguments on an excise tax proposal, or on the draft, or on the Vietnam War.

Perhaps convocation and commencement speeches have a built-in component which renders them more liable to criticism, or at least to mixed response. They are usually hortatory, and man is often perversely allergic to advice, however felicitously given. He would rather compose his own homilies than listen to someone else's.

The foregoing is not intended as a defense of the convocation speech. It needs none, for the superior specimens stand firmly on their own excellences. Teachers and students alike continue to receive inspiration and profit from the reading of addresses such as Robert F. Goheen's "The Library and the Chapel Stand Side by Side" (reprinted in *Representative American Speeches: 1964-1965,* pages 113-119), Edmund S. Morgan's "What Every Yale Freshman Should Know" and Jacques Barzun's "The Place and Price of Excellence" (both reprinted in Arnold, Ehninger, and Gerber's *The Speaker's Resource Book,* rev. ed., Chicago, Scott, 1966, pages 35-37 and 28-34, respectively).

[3] Dartmouth College, Hanover, New Hampshire, September 25, 1967. Text furnished by Mr. Dickey, with permission for this reprint.

[4] For biographical note, see Appendix.

John Sloan Dickey's address "The Betrayal of Idealism," delivered at a convocation at Dartmouth College on September 25, 1967, deservedly joins this list. For many years a distinguished lawyer and government official, Mr. Dickey has been president of Dartmouth since 1945.

A year ago on this occasion we discussed the educational imperative to bet our lives "on the daily double of high competence and . . . fulfillment as a man." The race to be human has never been run wholly on a fast track, but lately the going has been getting messier than it needs to be and certainly messier than it can be permitted to be if you are to have your chance at turning in a lifetime performance worthy of a highly educated man.

Paradoxically, it is both somewhat disturbing and yet rather reassuring to find that most of the things I propose to say today would have seemed to many of us until recently to go without saying. The French Foreign Minister, Maurice Couve de Murville, disposed of this problem in another connection with the decidedly un-French observation that "things that go without saying go even better if said."

Be that as it may, it will do no harm here for you and me to remind ourselves that we have been singled out by circumstance, chance and effort to be custodians and even, gentlemen, the embodiment of the best that over the ages man has discovered with his brain and defended with his life. And as men seeking liberation from all provincialisms, perhaps especially the provincialism of our own privilege, we also must have at least a vicarious awareness of what in the human situation is not right, and thereby has a claim on our conscience and our competence.

All this, of course, is the lifetime assignment of a liberating education. And given a lifetime with its spatial capacity for absorbing the human animal's early appetites, absolutes and impatience, civilized men and women have usually managed to raise their young without more than normal wear and tear on human institutions and with tolerable casualty lists in the perennial strife of different generations. Presumably this is still the long-run outlook as it has been the long run of the past. However, as some pragmatist has observed, in the long run we're all dead. You who must be young now or never and we who have bet our lives on your education cannot wait for the nirvana of the long run; we must run this lap in the race now or never.

The critical thing between teacher and student and, of course, between generations is what they have to say in all ways to each other. It is the interchange of experience and outlook that produces the sharing we call education. Youth has a 20-20 outlook which is great for seeing the big view; bifocals are not so good for great vistas, but they can help to keep experience in sight—and readable.

For my part I am now convinced that modern forces which we as yet very imperfectly understand have pried things loose the world around to a degree that now gives you and me unprecedented opportunities either to get forward constructively with man's great purposes or to mess things up with the thoroughness of a Greek tragedy made nightmarish by the contemporary cultists of irrationality.

It is often easier to see the other fellow's trash than our own and not many of us were surprised to have James Reston report from Havana last month that "the saddest thing about the Cuban revolution is that it is teaching hate and violence to the young." That's the way it's supposed to be in foreign countries where big, bad men with names such as Mussolini, Hitler, Stalin, Mao, and Castro led the ignorant, the weak and the gullible into the human swamps of fascism and communism where anything goes if it's for the cause—and anybody "goes" who isn't.

These movements have all professed idealistic objectives of a sort. What they have neither propounded nor practiced are those ideals of behavior that protect by law and conscience the right of the individual to have his say even as a minority of one, to have his way even as a majority of one, and to make his own way in the dignity of freedom and human equality.

Fascism and communism have surely spawned hate and violence, but let us especially not forget that in terrifying measure they were propounded and accepted as responses to the inevitable outcry for "law and order" in societies that had fallen prey to instigated riots, brawls and corruption through the failure of self-government, in one way or another, to govern.

If there are those—and in fact we know there are all too many—who are blind or indifferent to the imperfections and injustices of our society, particularly as it has imposed second-class citizenship on some 20 million Negro citizens, it will surely be no service to anyone, especially the poor and the disadvantaged, to permit, let alone foment, situations that in any civilized society will invoke the authority of raw power in response to the inevitable elemental call of the citizenry for "law and order."

There are, of course, those who either by reason of personal desperation or makeup cannot or will not be governed by such counsels of experience, and these people have a call on our understanding and compassion; but God forbid that the American academic community should find itself jockeyed into being a stalking horse for the proposition that in America today any cause can be well served by conduct that would be intolerable behavior if used by the Philistines on us.

If anyone hesitates to credit this possibility, he would do well to ponder the action of the annual congress of the National Student Association this summer at which, after an extensive and explicit debate about the place of violence in our public affairs and the dangerous implication of what was being proposed, a majority was won for a resolution endorsing "black power" defined as "the unification of all black peoples in America for their liberation by any means necessary." The crucial issue of the debate was an unsuccessful effort to delete the words *by any means necessary.*

Having begun my service in the cause of Negro "liberation" twenty years ago as a member of President Truman's historic Committee on Civil Rights and having won a few battle stars since then, I have no reason to be hesitant about saying that this kind of "provocative bluster" is a tragically ill-advised disservice to the cause of righting the worst wrong of America's proud history.

My main concern here today, however, is not with particular causes, even this great one; rather, it is with the overriding cause that this highly motivated college generation shall not discredit itself and the very ideals to which it is committed by losing its way in the swamp of human folly where anything goes if it's on your side. This swampland embraces every form of unworthiness from the unkindness of bad manners to the arrogance of justifying unprincipled behavior by one's ideals. "By any means necessary" is the swampland into which some of the nation's finest youthful talent was drawn and tragically lost during the decade of the thirties. It is the great folly of good intentions en route to their proverbial destiny. It is the betrayal of idealism.

More could be said, but I could not care more that your talent and your caring should not be lost to a future that you and your Dartmouth education could brighten.

As I read man's experience with civilization, no future is likely to be long lost that is paved with good ways as well as good intentions. And no other future can be well won.

Gentlemen, forget about civilization if you will, but do remember this: in all the years ahead few things will make more of a difference to you than the way other men deal with you in pursuing their ends, many of which you won't share.

And now, men of Dartmouth, since it does need saying, I urge each of you to be aware that as a member of the College you have three different but closely intertwined roles to play:

First, you are citizens of a community and are expected to act as such. Second, you are the stuff of an institution and what you are it will be. Thirdly, your business here is learning and that is up to you. We'll be with you all the way, and Good Luck!

DISSENT—1968 STYLE [5]

ERWIN N. GRISWOLD [6]

A wide gulf separates passive disagreement from the most virulent manifestations of civil disobedience. Yet they have some common elements, chief among them a displeasure with an existing condition or state of mind. Neither disagreement nor disobedience is new in American life; both have been very much a part of our record. Of the value of responsible disagreement and dissent, there should be little doubt; but when civil disobedience assumes menacing dimensions, serious moral and legal questions arise.

In a foregoing speech by Professor Daniel J. Boorstin, distinctions were drawn between disagreement and dissent. Similarly, other legal experts have differentiated dissent from civil disobedience. In his lecture on April 17, 1968, at the Syracuse University College of Law, Earl F. Morris, president of the American Bar Association, observed that "when protesters march on the sidewalk in front of an induction center to demonstrate peacefully their opposition to the war, this is dissent; but when people sit and lie in the street and block the access to traffic to that induction center, this is civil disobedience, and it is unlawful." Mr. Morris pointed out through selected examples, however, that he was not assessing the point of view or the wisdom of the end sought through the actions; he was concerned primarily with the methods employed to achieve the objectives.

Students of argumentation and public address have a special interest in the protest activities which are currently of wide concern in American life. Apart from the causes with which they are identified, the expressions of dissent are viable examples showing the diversified role of controversy in the democratic process. And in no address of the past year are the moral and legal implications of dissent more acutely delineated and analyzed than in Erwin N.

[5] Tulane University Law School, New Orleans, Louisiana, April 16, 1968. Text furnished by Mr. Griswold, with permission for this reprint. The lecture was printed in the June 1968 *Tulane Law Review:* Griswold, *Dissent 1968,* 42 Tul. L. Rev. 726 (1968). Permission to reprint granted by Billups P. Percy, faculty adviser to the Tulane Law Review Association.

[6] For biographical note, see Appendix.

Griswold's George Abel Dreyfous Lecture on Civil Liberties, delivered at the Tulane University School of Law on April 16, 1968.
Recently named the Solicitor General of the United States, Mr.
Griswold probes deftly and penetratingly the relation between
"recognition of the rights of conscience" as a basic assumption of
our society and the propriety of the method through which the
expression of conscience is exercised. Commenting on the sit-ins,
freedom rides, and other techniques used by civil rights groups in
the South, Mr. Griswold said:

> We cannot fail to recognize the fact that it was these tactics
> which succeeded in putting the basic issues squarely before
> the courts and the public. And it was in this way that the
> law was clarified in the courts and that legislative changes
> were brought about. . . .

> There are great lessons to be learned from this experience.
> Perhaps the greatest of these is that what mattered was not
> merely the moral fervor of the demonstrators, or the justice
> of their cause, but also the way in which they conducted
> themselves. They and their leaders were aware of the moral
> dimensions of their cause, and they knew that this required
> an equal adherence to morality in the means by which they
> sought to vindicate their cause. Because of this, rigid ad-
> herence to the philosophy of nonviolence was sought and
> widely achieved. In retrospect, I am sure that our nation will
> point with pride not only to the courage of those who risked
> punishment in order to challenge injustice, but also to the
> morality of their actions in scrupulously avoiding violence,
> even in reaction to the force which was exerted on them.
> The affirmation of the close relation between morality and
> nonviolence will be one of the many monuments of the Rev.
> Martin Luther King, Jr.

In addition to this lecture by the former Dean of the Harvard
Law School, interested students will find the following items on
dissent particularly helpful and provocative: the widely heralded
paperback *Concerning Dissent and Civil Disobedience* by Associate
Justice of the Supreme Court Abe Fortas; the William H. Gifford
Memorial Lecture entitled "American Society and the Rebirth of
Civil Disobedience," delivered at the Syracuse University College
of Law on April 17, 1968, by Earl F. Morris, president of the
American Bar Association; and "On Civil Disobedience, 1967," a
collection of observations by thirteen scholars and writers on the
limits of civil disobedience and related themes, in the New York
Times Magazine, November 26, 1967, pages 27-29 +.

Preserving civil peace is the first responsibility of government.[7]

Unfortunately, since the populace has been sluggish and complacent, occasional violence seems to be advantageous to wake people up. . . .[8]

When I first accepted the invitation to deliver this year's Dreyfous Lecture, it was my intention to discuss, in a rather abstract way, some of the changes that have taken place in the modes of dissent over the years. The sad events of the past ten days, however, have led me to revise my emphasis somewhat. Rather than recite the changes of the past, I wish to speak to you tonight about some fundamental postulates of our democratic society, principles which I believe must be kept in vivid focus and which must be meaningfully communicated to the community as a whole if true freedom—not frenetic license—is to endure.

Let me begin by confessing that I am aware that between the polar extremes which I shall discuss there are confusing overlays of principle and policy and there will remain very substantial areas where the conscientious judgment of the informed individual is the only operative standard. But for the individual to make a rational choice, he must be aware of the values and consequences at stake when he forms his conscience and determines to follow it, and it is in the hope that it will encourage reflective appreciation of what is truly involved in *civil disobedience*—which has become the most pervasive contemporary aspect of civil liberties—that I submit these remarks for your attention.

I

Ambassador Sol M. Linowitz touched on the core of the problem in his address last month before a conference organized by the American Assembly and the American Bar Association when he suggested that in recent years there has

[7] *Report of the National Advisory Commission on Civil Disorders* 171 (March 1, 1968).

[8] Goodman, "The Resisters Support U.S. Traditions and Interests," in *On Civil Disobedience, 1967*, New York *Times Magazine*, November 26, 1967, p. 124.

been a material change in the public attitude toward law. He observed that law is now too often viewed "not as the living model for a free society, but rather as a mode of callous repression, or—no less disturbingly—as a collection of precatory suggestions which can be flouted or ignored." [9]

The focus of these remarks, just as with the Ambassador's observation, is not professional crime engaged in by those who are indifferent to legal obstacles to their own enrichment. What is of more concern is that our society has become increasingly tolerant of the mischievous attempts to excuse deliberate violations of the law committed in furtherance of what the actor personally regards as a lofty cause. I shall advert later on to justifiable examples of civil disobedience, but what I suggest is that intellectual and practical consequence of indiscriminate civil disobedience is the "legitimation of violence" of which we have seen too much in America. I borrow this phrase from the recent Presidential Riot Commission, which listed this sorry fact of American society as one of the basic causes of riots. The Commission's conclusion, under this heading is as follows: [10]

A climate that tends toward the approval and encouragement of violence as a form of protest has been created by white terrorism directed against nonviolent protest, including instances of abuse and even murder of some civil rights workers in the South, by the open defiance of law and Federal authority by state and local officials resisting desegregation, and by some protest groups engaging in civil disobedience who turn their backs on nonviolence, go beyond constitutionally protected rights of petition and free assembly and resort to violence to attempt to compel alteration of laws and policies with which they disagree. This condition has been reenforced by a general erosion of respect for authority in American society and the reduced effectiveness of social standards and community restraints on violence and crime.

The ink is not yet dry on the latest confirmation of this conclusion. The almost inevitable retaliation that the Com-

[9] "Some Reflections on the Challenges to Lawyers and the Law," March 16, 1968.
[10] *Report of the National Advisory Commission on Civil Disorders* 92 (March 1, 1968).

mission spoke of was not long in coming, and over a hundred cities have been wracked by the manifestation of grim, mindless destruction. To argue that massive retaliation against society at large is both unjustifiable and self-defeating [11]— while unquestionably correct—misses the point that our national temperament has become too much acclimated to violence as a method of social protest.

Perhaps you may interject that no one who champions the right of protest in general, or the privilege of civil disobedience in particular, would seek to justify either political assassinations or riots. Of course I would not dispute this caveat, but the troubling circumstances I have sketched have both a logical and a practical relevance to issues of protest and dissent. They are logically related to our focus because they represent the ultimate mode of dissent—rejection not merely of the position of the majority but of the very foundation of civilized society itself: Civil Order. They have a practical impact on our topic too, for these extreme acts I have adverted to are in a sense the product of the same undiscriminating and uncritical attitude toward individual choice about the binding nature of law that underlies less dramatic but similarly irresponsible forms of protest.

II

We Americans have always taken a considerable measure of pride in our personal independence and right to nonconformity. But in my view, effective self-government is nevertheless the greatest achievement of mankind. I trust that most Americans share the conclusion that government is not merely inevitable but highly desirable. And from this axiom, certain corollaries flow.

The *first* of these is, I think that civil disobedience differs quite radically in important respects from ordinary modes of protest and dissent. The crucial attribute of civil disobedience is that it is expressed through deliberate violation of

[11] *E.g.*, Leibman. *Civil Disobedience: A Threat to Our Law Society*, 51 A.B.A.J. 645, 646 (1965).

the law.[12] Read in the context of its origin, the First Amendment not only creates a right to dissent but in a very real sense encourages the exercise of this prerogative. That is why we are concerned about "chilling" First Amendment freedoms. But our law and custom have long been clear that the right to differ with society and to reject its code of behavior has limits, and the First Amendment will not do service to sanction every sort of activity that is sought to be justified as an expression of nonconformity.

Second, equally important and sometimes profoundly troubling, our political tradition has long recognized that a man's abiding duty to his conscience transcends his obligation to the State. Chief Justice Hughes once put it this way:[13]

Much has been said of the paramount duty to the State, a duty to be recognized, it is urged, even though it conflicts with convictions of duty to God. Undoubtedly that duty to the State exists within the domain of power, for government may enforce obedience to laws regardless of scruples. When one's belief collides with the power of the State, the latter is supreme within its sphere and submission or punishment follows. But, in the forum of conscience, duty to a moral power higher than the State has always been maintained.

Third, in a democracy such as ours, each individual shares both a political and a moral duty "actively to participate—to some degree, at least—in the processes of government and law-making." I am quoting the words of my friend, Professor J. N. D. Anderson of the University of London.[14] He continues: "In a democracy, indeed, every citizen bears a measure of personal responsibility for misgovernment, bad laws, or wrong policies, unless he has played his full part in trying to get a better government into power, better laws on the statute book, and better policies adopted."

[12] One of the more thoughtful analyses of this topic is that given by Dean Francis Allen in *Civil Disobedience and the Legal Order,* 36 U. Cin. L. Rev. 1, 175 (1967).

[13] *United States v. Macintosh,* 283 U.S. 605, 633 (Hughes, C.J., and Holmes, Brandeis, and Stone, JJ., dissenting).

[14] Anderson, *Into the World—the Need and Limits of Christian Involvement* 41 (London, 1968).

As my *fourth* corollary, and here perhaps I will meet with slightly less universal agreement, I suggest that what we have been classically concerned about protecting is the dissemination of ideas—protecting the individual's access to the intellectual market place where he may offer his conception of the ills and remedies for social or political problems. Thus, historically, our motivation and our objective have been the attempt to encourage the search for truth or wisdom, or both. To quote Chief Justice Hughes again:[15]

The maintenance of the opportunity for free political discussion to the end that government may be responsive to the will of the people and that changes may be obtained by lawful means, an opportunity essential to the security of the republic, is a fundamental principle of our constitutional system.

Given these principles, which I regard as not merely orthodox but sound, let me turn to the forms of dissent and protest which are currently the vogue so that we may proceed to consider some of the problems of dissent and in particular of civil disobedience.

III

Toward the end of the last century, Justice Holmes observed that on the basis of his experience, "Behind every scheme to make the world over, lies the question, What kind of world do you want?" [16] It may well have been true in those times that dissent and protest and agitation—for women's suffrage, or prohibition, or socialism, or anarchism, or whatever—had a more or less conscious and systematic design for the objective which was sought to be achieved. But today, much protest seems reflexive rather than cerebral, motivated more by the desire to reject established positions and policies than by deliberate preference for some alternatives. Perhaps I am not perceptive enough to discern the latent wisdom and goals of movements that seek the elevation of

[15] *Stromberg v. California*, 283 U.S. 359, 369.
[16] *The Occasional Speeches of Justice Oliver Wendell Holmes* 75 (Howe ed. 1962).

dirty words on campus, or that exalt the virtues of "flower power," or that conduct a "strip-in" in a public park. The message, if there is one, escapes me.

We have in this country, of course, recognized that the display of symbols as an expression of some dissenting position is entitled to constitutional protection. That was settled as long ago at least as the "red flag" case.[17] But all this presupposes that there is some intelligible and definable nexus between the form of the protest and what is being protested. Thus, when a prominent New York couple several years ago decided to express their indignation at increased municipal taxes by stringing clotheslines draped with rags and tattered uniforms in their front yard, the state courts found this "bizarre" manner of symbolic dissent unprotected, with Judge Stanley Fuld writing that it was clear that the "value of their 'protest' lay not in its message but in its offensiveness."[18] And the Supreme Court summarily ruled that their claims of "free speech" were in the circumstances clearly frivolous.

I have similar difficulty with other popular forms of modern "dissent." Have we reached the point in this country where anything is contributed to our shared desire for progress and achievement by "writing dirty words on a fence about the President of the country? Or calling members of his Administration names?"[19] No less prominent a spokesman for dissent than Bayard Rustin has expressed his "puzzlement" at the tactics employed by some young people in proclaiming their disenchantment with present conditions. He remarks rather pointedly that he is "concerned about their believing that you can educate people on the basis of simplistic slogans . . . rather than on the basis of a concrete program of concrete recommendations."[20] While satire and

[17] *Stromberg v. California,* 283 U.S. 359. Compare *West Virginia State Board of Education v. Barnette,* 319 U.S. 624.

[18] *People v. Stover,* 12 N.Y. 2d 462, 470, 240 N.Y.S. 2d 734, 191 N.E. 2d 272 (1963), appeal dismissed, 375 U.S. 42.

[19] Farrell, "Today's Disobedience Is Uncivil," in *On Civil Disobedience, 1967,* New York *Times Magazine,* November 26, 1967, p. 29.

[20] Rustin, in *Civil Disobedience* 10 (Center for the Study of Democratic Institutions 1966).

sharp rapier thrusts have long been among the accepted, and effective, modes of social and political criticism, I doubt that personal ridicule or broad-gauge contumely has ever produced light rather than heat, or constructively contributed to the resolution of major questions.

I do not question the constitutional right to be irrelevant or intemperate or even unfair. Our jurisprudence has made it clear that it is a prerogative of American citizenship "to criticize public men and measures—and that means not only informed and responsible criticism but the freedom to speak foolishly and without moderation." [21] In part this is the consequence of the assumption of our democratic system that the people can be trusted to test competing ideas and proposals, after free discussion, and "to withstand ideas that are wrong." [22] And in part it reflects our policy that even damaging and false assertions, and those unrelated to alternative programs, must be suffered lest the submission of important and constructive suggestions be deterred.[23]

IV

There is a contemporary aspect of the problem to which, I think, too little attention has been given.

When our basic notions of freedom of speech, and of the right to dissent, were developed—largely in the eighteenth century—communication was very different from what it is now. There were fewer people—only three million in the United States. Most of them were close to the soil, and many were not unduly literate. The market place for political ideas was more limited than it is now.

Perhaps of even greater importance, though, was the fact that the speed of communication of ideas was very slow. Freedom of speech and press meant freedom for Thomas Paine to publish "Common Sense," or for John Adams to

[21] *Baumgartner v. United States*, 322 U.S. 665, 673-674. See also *Bridges v. California*, 314 U.S. 252.

[22] *Barenblatt v. United States*, 360 U.S. 109, 146 (Black, J. dissenting).

[23] See generally *New York Times Co. v. Sullivan*, 376 U.S. 254.

write an article for a newspaper and for the newspaper to publish it. When these and other things were printed, they were read in the privacy of the home, with few other persons around. Ideas had an opportunity to percolate, to be examined and considered, and to be refined and reformed in the thoughts of the people.

Of course, there was speech making, too. But one person's voice could reach perhaps a thousand people, perhaps somewhat more under very special circumstances. The speech could, of course, be printed, but it would be the next day before it was read in the same community, and days or weeks before it was read elsewhere. Almost always, there was time for thoughtful consideration. Moreover, the volume of material which was communicated, in print or by speech, was very limited. There was adequate opportunity for thoughtful people to comprehend, to absorb, and digest. In the modern world, though, this has been changed completely. The change has been developing over the years, with the telegraph and telephone, and the speed of transportation. With the coming of the radio, it was possible for President Roosevelt to address fifty or one hundred million people at once, with an impact that had never been known before.

In recent years, the facilities of communication have continued to develop until our situation is utterly different from what it was even a generation ago. In older days, a person who had an idea to express—whether of dissent, or otherwise, had some difficulty in bringing this about. To publish it in a book or pamphlet might be beyond his means. There were few newspapers, and these did not have much space. Unless the idea was extremely good, or well expressed, it was not likely that a newspaper could be found to publish it.

Today, however, the news media are avid for news. Television stations are putting out news through all the hours of the day, and they are always seeking something new or different, something that will attract viewers to their station. Almost anyone who wants to do something bizarre on a public street can find his way on television, and be seen by millions or tens of millions of people all over the country, and, indeed, through much of the world.

Because the newspapers are in competition with the television stations, they have to present the same news. Thus, there has been an enormous increase in the opportunity to express dissent, and, perhaps even more important, an even greater increase in the immediacy of dissent and the impact which it can make. There may be real room to question whether we have psychologically caught up with the developments in communications' speed and distribution, whether we are capable of absorbing and evaluating all of the materials which are now communicated daily to hundreds of millions of people.

I do not mean to suggest that the communications agencies have acted irresponsibly. They, too, have had to learn their power while the public was beginning to become aware of it. There are clear signs that television and newspapers are aware of their responsibilities in these areas, and are accepting them. There is a hard line for them to follow. For they must serve the ideals of a free press. Yet, all of the problems are enormously magnified, and the essential nature of responsibility in the exercise of a free press stands out more clearly as the magnification increases. The power of communication, through press, radio and television, has become an awesome power. Its use is essential to the preservation of a free society. Only time will tell, I suppose, whether our system can adequately adjust itself to the impact of modern communications methods. I am only trying to point out here the importance of the exercise of responsibility in the expression of dissent in the modern world.

V

We must draw two fundamental distinctions when we speak of dissent; the first involves primarily legal and moral variables and divides permissible from unpermissible dissent; the second presupposes that the dissent is tolerable but involves the social and political considerations of whether, or

when or how the protest *should* be made. The latter is not
a question of right, but of judgment and morals, even of
taste, and a proper sense of restraint and responsibility, qualities which are or should be inherent in the very concept of
civil liberties.

We must begin any analysis of these questions with the
undoubted fact that we live in a society, an imperfect and
struggling one no doubt, but one where government and
order are not only a necessity but are the preference of an
overwhelming majority of the citizenry. The rules that society has developed to organize and order itself are found in a
body of law which has not been imposed from outside, but
has been slowly built up from experience expressed through
the consent of the governed, and now pervades all aspects of
human activity. Inevitably there are occasions when individuals or groups will chafe under a particular legal bond, or
will bridle in opposition to a particular governmental policy, and the question presents itself, what can be done?

Vocal objection, of course—even slanderous or inane—is
permissible. But the fact that one is a dissenter with a right
to express his opposition entitles him to no special license.
Thus, in expressing views that are themselves wholly immune
to official strictures he gains no roving commission to ignore
the rules and underlying assumption of society that relate in
a neutral way to activity rather than to the maintenance or
expression of ideas. Thus, I submit that one cannot rightly
engage in conduct which is otherwise unlawful merely because he intends that either that conduct or the idea he
wishes to express in the course of the conduct is intended to
manifest his dissent from some governmental policy. I cannot distinguish in principle the legal quality of the determination to halt a troop train to protest the Vietnam war or
to block workmen from entering a segregated job site to protest employment discrimination, from the determination to
fire shots into a civil rights leader's home to protest integration. The right to disagree—and to manifest disagreement—
which the Constitution allows to the individuals in those situ-

ations—does not authorize them to carry on their campaign of education and persuasion at the expense of someone else's liberty, or in violation of some laws whose independent validity is unquestionable.

This distinction runs deep in our history, but has too frequently been ignored in this decade. But the line is a clear one, and we should reestablish it in the thinking and understanding of our people. While I share Professor Harry Kalven's assessment that the "generosity and empathy with which [public streets and parks] are made available [as a "public forum"] is an index of freedom,[24] I regard as unassailable the limitation that the mere fact that a person wishes to make a public point does not sanction any method he chooses to use to make it. Yet there seems to be currently a considerable tendency to ignore if not to reject this limitation. Certainly many of the modern forms of dissent, including those I have just mentioned, proceed on the basis of the contrary proposition. Only last Term the Supreme Court was asked to sustain the right of demonstrators active in a cause that most of us here and the Court itself no doubt regarded as laudable, to lodge their demand for an end to segregation on the grounds of a city jail where, it seemed, biased treatment was being accorded prisoners. The argument was made that a demonstration at that site was "particularly appropriate," irrespective of the consequences. Speaking for the Court, Justice Black rejected this rationale, explaining that [25]

Such an argument has as its major unarticulated premise the assumption that people who want to propagandize protests or views have a constitutional right to do so whenever and however and wherever they please.

That notion the Court expressly "vigorously and forthrightly rejected."

Another form of protest that can never, in my view, be excused or tolerated, is that which assumes the posture of a

[24] Kalven, *The Concept of the Public Forum: Cox v. Louisiana,* 1965 Supreme Court Review 12.

[25] *Adderley v. Florida,* 385 U.S. 39, 47-48.

violent and forcible assault on public order, whatever the motivation. The interests at stake in such a situation must transcend the validity of the particular cause and the permissibility of adhering to it. Violent opposition to law—any law—or forcible disregard of another's freedom to disagree falls beyond the pale of legitimate dissent or even of civil disobedience, properly understood; it is nothing short of rebellion.

The utter indefensibility of violent opposition to law is that it proceeds on the foolhardy and immoral principle that might makes right. Centuries ago Rousseau rejected this approach as a viable political alternative:[26]

For, if force creates right, the effect changes with the cause: every force that is greater than the first succeeds to its right. As soon as it is possible to disobey with impunity, disobedience is legitimate; and, the strongest being always in the right, the only thing that matters is to act so as to become the strongest. But what kind of right is that which perishes when force fails?

To permit factions the resort to force when they feel—however correctly—that a particular law or policy is wrong would be to renounce our own experience and that of the Founders. In support of this view, I offer two sentences written by Justice Frankfurter: "Law alone saves a society from being rent by internecine strife or ruled by mere brute power however disguised."[27] And, "Violent resistance to law cannot be made a legal reason for its suspension without loosening the fabric of our society."[28]

What is at stake is not mere order but also the lessons of history. True freedom and substantial justice come not from violent altercations or incendiary dissent. "No mob has ever protected any liberty, even its own."[29] While the First Amendment embodies a distrust of the collective conscience of the majority in areas of fundamental liberty, it no more

[26] *The Social Contract*, Bk. I, Chapter 3.

[27] *United States v. United Mine Workers*, 330 U.S. 258, 308.

[28] *Cooper v. Aaron*, 358 U.S. 1, 22.

[29] *Terminiello v. Chicago*, 337 U.S. 1, 32 (Jackson, J., dissenting).

intended to leave the limits of freedom to the judgment of coercive dissenters. "Civil government cannot let any group ride rough-shod over others simply because their 'consciences' tell them to do so."[30]

VI

These reflections have dealt with the question when law and government may tolerate dissent, or dissent manifested in certain ways, and I have suggested that it is illicit to violate otherwise valid laws either as a symbol of protest or in the course of protest, and secondly that I regard it as indefensible to attempt to promote a viewpoint either by flagrant violence or by organized coercion. Now I will turn finally to the second distinction to which I referred earlier in this lecture. That is, assuming a legal or moral right to protest, what considerations of prudence and responsibility should infuse the determination to exercise these rights.

First, you will note that I imply that a line may be drawn between legal and moral rights to dissent. I am not now referring to what I accept as the genuine possibility that one may exercise his constitutional right to dissent in a way that, because of recklessness or unfairness, makes his conduct ethically improper. I mention this distinction, however, because I believe awareness and evaluation of it should always be taken into account in considering an exercise of the right to dissent. But for the present, I mean to concentrate on the converse of this distinction, that there may be a moral right to dissent without a corresponding legal privilege to do so. It is in this context that "civil disobedience" must be viewed.

Earlier, I observed that our system contemplates that there may be a moral right to "civil disobedience" (properly understood) that exists notwithstanding a "legal" duty to obey. I also referred to the source of this moral right: the ultimate sanctity of a man's own conscience, as the intellectual and volitional composite that governs his conception of

[30] *Douglas v. City of Jeanette*, 319 U.S. 157, 179 (opinion of Jackson, J.)

his relation to Eternal Truth. I wish now to emphasize the considerations which, in my view, condition the existence and exercise of this moral right, because I believe the current rhetoric—which sometimes seems to consecrate "civil disobedience" as the noblest response in the pantheon of virtues—has obscured the nature and consequence of this activity. To define my term—I mean by "civil disobedience" the deliberate violation of a rule ordained by constituted government because of a conscientious conviction that the law is so unjust that it cannot morally be observed by the individual.

The most important point to be stressed is that this decision is one that should be made only after the most painful and introspective reflection, and only when the firm conclusion is reached that obedience offends the most fundamental personal values. It is self-evident that routine or random noncompliance with the law for transient or superficial reasons would negate the first principles of civilized behavior. Unless society can safely assume that *almost* without exception individuals will accept the will of the majority even when to do so is grudging and distasteful, the foundation of secure liberty will rather rapidly erode. John Locke, who in his profound *Letter Concerning Toleration* analyzed and defended the right of obedience to conscience over civil law in case of severe conflict, thereafter cautioned in his essay *Concerning Civil Government*:[31]

May [the sovereign] be resisted, as often as any one shall find himself aggrieved, and but imagine he has not right done him? This will unhinge and overturn all polities, and instead of government and order, leave nothing but anarchy and confusion.

Last year, in delivering this Lecture, Arthur Goodhart observed, "Thus, it has been correctly said that obedience to the law is a major part of patriotism."[32] He meant this not as a castigation of dissent or as an outburst of flag-waving chauvinism, but rather as a formulation of a central political

[31] Chapter XVIII, paragraph 203.
[32] *Recognition of the Binding Nature of Law*, 41 Tul. L. Rev. 769, 773 (1967).

truth: That if human society is to enjoy freedom, it cannot tolerate license. Henry David Thoreau is generally regarded as the most notable American exponent of civil disobedience, and all of us share admiration for his determination. But we must not ignore the vital aspect of Thoreau's nonconformity —his passionate attempt to dissociate himself from society. He was, as Harry Kalven has put it, "a man who does not see himself as belonging very intensely to the community in which he was raised,"[33] and who sought constantly but futilely to reject the society to which he had not voluntarily adhered.

Thoreau's poignant attitude was charming enough in mid-nineteenth century America. But it was, essentially, an effort to withdraw from the realities of life and it was, I suggest, myopic even then, for it was painfully inconsistent with the fact that man is a part of society by nature, by geography, and by citizenship. Unlike a member of a purely artificial group, like a bar association or country club, a citizen cannot resign from the "social compact" because he protests policies of the regime. Now in the last third of the twentieth century, we must be even more cognizant that there is nothing noble or salutary about foredoomed attempts to abdicate membership in society. Complex problems demand rational attention that can come only from personal focus on solutions and never from stubbornly turning one's back on harsh and unpleasant realities.

This is precisely what nonconformity as a way of life is. It is the essential irrationality of the "hippie movement"—a mass endeavor to drop out of life. It is a protest of sorts, of course, but one that can bear no fruit, because it takes issue with what is not only inevitable, but more importantly, indispensable—social regulation of individual behavior.

Stretched to its logical extreme, this also is civil disobedience, and for this reason I urge that before any man embarks upon a unilateral nullification of any law he must

[33] "On Thoreau" in *Civil Disobedience* 25, 28 (Center for the Study of Democratic Institutions 1966).

appreciate that his judgment has not merely a personal significance but also portends grave consequences for his fellows.

In determining whether and when to exercise the moral
right to disobey the dictates of the law, it must also be recognized that society not only does not but cannot recognize this
determination as entitled to legal privilege. It is part of the
Gandhian tradition of civil disobedience that the sincerity
of the individual's conscience presupposes that the law will
punish this assertion of personal principle. In the very for-
mation of our country, in the *Federalist* Papers, Hamilton
explained the reason why government cannot compromise
its authority by offering a dispensation for individual conscience:[34]

> Government implies the power of making laws. It is essential
> to the idea of a law, that it be attended with a sanction; or, in
> other words, a penalty or punishment for disobedience. If there
> be no penalty annexed to disobedience, the resolutions or com-
> mands which pretend to be laws will, in fact, amount to nothing
> more than advice or recommendation.

Thus, it is of the essence of law that it is equally applied
to all, that it binds all alike, irrespective of personal motive.
For this reason, one who contemplates civil disobedience out
of moral conviction should not be surprised and must not be
bitter if a criminal conviction ensues. And he must accept
the fact that organized society cannot endure on any other
basis. His hope is that he may aid in getting the law changed.
But if he does not succeed in that, he cannot complain if the
law is applied to him.

VII

Though I speak with seriousness about civil disobedience,
I hope that my remarks are not misunderstood. I endeavored
to make it plain in my opening analysis that a proper recognition of the rights of conscience is one of the basic assump-
tions of our society. The problem, of course, is to determine

[34] *The Federalist, Number 15.*

what is "proper." Like all questions worth discussing, it is inevitably one of degree.

In considering this question, it is well to examine not only *whether* civil disobedience is appropriate in a particular situation, but also *how* it is to be carried out. We have a vivid illustration of this in the experience of this generation. We are all aware of the fact that for many long years the legal structure was often used to perpetuate deprivations which were at odds with the most basic constitutional and moral values. During this time, conditions of political, social, and economic inequality made ineffective meaningful attempts to change these regulations and policies by petition within the customary channels of reform. In this situation, the only realistic recourse was deliberate refusal to abide by the restrictions any longer. Lunch-counter sit-ins and freedom rides are among the most dramatic examples of the techniques that were used to expose the injustices that were perpetrated under the banner of law. In many of these cases, these actions were not, indeed, illegal, since the restrictive laws were plainly invalid if one had the time, energy, and money to take them up to higher courts. In other cases, though, the line was not clear, and sometimes the actions taken were undoubtedly illegal. We cannot fail to recognize the fact that it was these tactics which succeeded in putting the basic issues squarely before the courts and the public. And it was in this way that the law was clarified in the courts and that legislative changes were brought about.

There are great lessons to be learned from this experience. Perhaps the greatest of these is that what mattered was not merely the moral fervor of the demonstrators, or the justice of their cause, but also the way in which they conducted themselves. They and their leaders were aware of the moral dimensions of their cause, and they knew that this required an equal adherence to morality in the means by which they sought to vindicate their cause. Because of this, rigid adherence to the philosophy of nonviolence was sought and widely achieved. In retrospect, I am sure that our nation will point with pride not only to the courage of those who risked punishment in order to challenge injustice, but also to the morality of their actions in scrupulously avoiding violence, even in reaction to the force which was exerted on them. The affirmation of the close relation between morality and non-violence will be one of the many monuments of the Rev. Martin Luther King, Jr.

As this experience shows, the ultimate legal success as well as the intrinsic moral quality of civil disobedience turns on the restraint with which it is exercised. This is an extremely hard line to draw, but it is one which must be earnestly sought out. Unfortunately, some of those who claim this mantle today do not appreciate the moral quality of thought and action which made their predecessors worthy to wear it.

Of course, it has not been my intention to disparage the objectives of any individual or group, or to discourage the honest and forthright and candid prophylaxis and therapy that are the legacy of reflective and constructive criticism. My only concern has been that some contemporary forms and philosophies of protest may in fact unwittingly retard the improvements in society which we all seek. I hope the ideas I have sought to present here may contribute to the thoughtful consideration of critical issues with which we must all deal in the creative evolution of our cherished land.

IN MEMORY OF GREATNESS

EULOGY ON DR. MARTIN LUTHER KING, JR.[1]

BENJAMIN E. MAYS [2]

On April 9, 1968, Dr. Martin Luther King, Jr. was buried in Atlanta. The funeral services in his memory began shortly after 10:30 A.M. at Ebenezer Baptist Church, where he and his father had shared the pulpit. The Rev. Ralph D. Abernathy, successor to the presidency of the Southern Christian Leadership Conference, conducted the services at which short tributes were delivered by the Rev. Ronald English, assistant pastor of Dr. King's church, and Dr. L. Harold DeWolfe, dean of Wesley Theological Seminary in Washington, D.C.

A cortege headed by the mule-drawn wagon bearing the coffin of Dr. King, and followed by thousands of mourners, then moved through the streets of the city to the campus of Morehouse College, where Dr. King received his bachelor's degree in 1948. In an impressive ceremony attended by many of America's most distinguished citizens, Dr. Benjamin H. Mays, president emeritus of Morehouse College, delivered the formal eulogy on Dr. King.

He belonged to the world and to mankind, [said Dr. Mays]. Now he belongs to posterity. . . .

If physical death was the price he had to pay to rid America of prejudice and injustice, nothing could be more redemptive. And, to paraphrase the words of the immortal John Fitzgerald Kennedy, permit me to say that Martin Luther King, Jr.'s unfinished work on earth must truly be our own.

To be honored by being requested to give the eulogy at the funeral of Dr. Martin Luther King, Jr. is like asking one to eulogize his deceased son—so close and so precious was he to me. Our friendship goes back to his student days at More-

[1] Morehouse College, Atlanta, Georgia, April 9, 1968. Text furnished by Dr. Mays, with permission for this reprint. (The press of the crowds and physical and emotional fatigue began to take their toll when the services got under way about 3:00 P.M. Accordingly, Dr. Mays cut about five minutes from his prepared text.)

[2] For biographical note, see Appendix.

house College. It is not an easy task; nevertheless I accept it, with a sad heart and with full knowledge of my inadequacy to do justice to this man. It was my desire that if I predeceased Dr. King, he would pay tribute to me on my final day. It was his wish that if he predeceased me, I would deliver the homily at his funeral. Fate has decreed that I eulogize him. I wish it might have been otherwise; for, after all, I am three score years and ten and Martin Luther is dead at thirty-nine.

Although there are some who rejoice in his death, there are millions across the length and breadth of this world who are smitten with grief that this friend of mankind—all mankind—has been cut down in the flower of his youth. So, multitudes here and in foreign lands, queens, kings, heads of governments, the clergy of the world, and the common man everywhere, are praying that God will be with the family, the American people, and the President of the United States in this tragic hour. We hope that this universal concern will bring comfort to the family—for grief is like a heavy load: when shared it is easier to bear. We come today to help the family carry the load.

We have assembled here from every section of this great nation and from other parts of the world to give thanks to God that He gave to America, at this moment in history, Martin Luther King, Jr. Truly God is no respecter of persons. How strange! God called the grandson of a slave on his father's side, and the grandson of a man born during the Civil War on his mother's side, and said to him: Martin Luther, speak to America about war and peace; about social justice and racial discrimination; about its obligation to the poor; and about nonviolence as a way of perfecting social change in a world of brutality and war.

Here was a man who believed with all of his might that the pursuit of violence at any time is ethically and morally wrong; that God and the moral weight of the universe are against it; that violence is self-defeating; and that only love and forgiveness can break the vicious circle of revenge. He believed that nonviolence would prove effective in the abolition of injustice in politics, in economics, in education, and in race relations. He was convinced, also, that people could not be moved to abolish voluntarily the inhumanity of man to man by mere persuasion and pleading, but that they could be moved to do so by dramatizing the evil through massive nonviolent resistance. He believed that nonviolent direct action was necessary to supplement the nonviolent victories won in the Federal courts. He believed that the nonviolent approach to solving social problems would ultimately prove to be redemptive.

Out of this conviction, history records the marches in Montgomery, Birmingham, Selma, Chicago, and other cities. He gave people an ethical and moral way to engage in activities designed to perfect social change without bloodshed and violence; and when violence did erupt it was that which is potential in any protest which aims to uproot deeply entrenched wrongs. No reasonable person would deny that the activities and the personality of Martin Luther King, Jr. contributed largely to the success of the student sit-in movements in abolishing segregation in downtown establishments; and that his activities contributed mightily to the passage of the Civil Rights legislation of 1964 and 1965.

Martin Luther King, Jr. believed in a united America. He believed that the walls of separation brought on by legal and de facto segregation, and discrimination based on race and color, could be eradicated. As he said in his Washington Monument address: "I have a dream."

He had faith in his country. He died striving to desegregate and integrate America to the end that this great nation of ours, born in revolution and blood, conceived in liberty and dedicated to the proposition that all men are created free and equal, will truly become the lighthouse of freedom where none will be denied because his skin is black and none favored because his eyes are blue; where our nation will be militarily strong but perpetually at peace; economically secure but just; learned but wise; where the poorest—the gar-

bage collectors—will have bread enough and to spare; where
no one will be poorly housed; each educated up to his capacity; and where the richest will understand the meaning
of empathy. *This* was his dream, and the end toward which
he strove. As he and his followers so often sang: "We shall
overcome someday; black and white together."

Let it be thoroughly understood that our deceased brother
did not embrace nonviolence out of fear or cowardice. Moral
courage was one of his noblest virtues. As Mahatma Gandhi
challenged the British Empire without a sword and won,
Martin Luther King, Jr. challenged the interracial wrongs
of his country without a gun. And he had the faith to believe
that he would win the battle for social justice. I make bold
to assert that it took more courage for King to practice nonviolence than it took his assassin to fire the fatal shot. The
assassin is a coward: he committed his dastardly deed and
fled. When Martin Luther disobeyed an unjust law, he accepted the consequences of his actions. He never ran away
and he never begged for mercy. He returned to the Birmingham jail to serve his time.

Perhaps he was more courageous than soldiers who fight
and die on the battlefield. There is an element of compulsion
in their dying. But when Martin Luther faced death again
and again, and finally embraced it, there was no external
pressure. He was acting on an inner compulsion that drove
him on. More courageous than those who advocate violence
as a way out, for they carry weapons of destruction for defense. But Martin Luther faced the dogs, the police, jail,
heavy criticism, and finally death; and he never carried a
gun, not even a knife to defend himself. He had only his
faith in a just God to rely on; and the belief that "thrice is
he armed who has his quarrels just." The faith that Brown-
ing writes about when he says:

> One who never turned his back but marched breast
>   forward,
> Never doubted clouds would break,

Never dreamed, though right were worsted, wrong
would triumph,
Held we fall to rise, and baffled to fight better,
Sleep to wake.

Coupled with moral courage was Martin Luther King, Jr.'s capacity to love people. Though deeply committed to a program of freedom for Negroes, he had love and concern for all kinds of peoples. He drew no distinction between the high and the low; none between the rich and the poor. He believed especially that he was sent to champion the cause of the man farthest down. He would probably say that if death had to come, I am sure there was no greater cause to die for than fighting to get a just wage for garbage collectors. He was supra-race, supra-nation, supra-denomination, supra-class, and supra-culture. He belonged to the world and to mankind. Now he belongs to posterity.

But there is a dichotomy in all this. This man was loved by some and hated by others. If any man knew the meaning of suffering, King knew. House bombed; living day by day for thirteen years under constant threats of death; maliciously accused of being a Communist; falsely accused of being insincere and seeking the limelight for his own glory; stabbed by a member of his own race; slugged in a hotel lobby; jailed thirty times; occasionally deeply hurt because friends betrayed him—and yet this man had no bitterness in his heart, no rancor in his soul, no revenge in his mind; and he went up and down the length and breadth of this world preaching nonviolence and the redemptive power of love. He believed with all of his heart, mind, and soul that the way to peace and brotherhood is through nonviolence, love, and suffering. He was severely criticized for his opposition to the war in Vietnam. It must be said, however, that one could hardly expect a prophet of Dr. King's commitments to advocate nonviolence at home and violence in Vietnam. Nonviolence to King was total commitment not only in solving the problems of race in the United States but in solving the problems of the world.

Surely this man was called of God to do this work. If
Amos and Micah were prophets in the eighth century B.C.,
Martin Luther King, Jr. was a prophet in the twentieth
century. If Isaiah was called of God to prophesy in his day,
Martin Luther was called of God to prophesy in his time.
If Hosea was sent to preach love and forgiveness centuries
ago, Martin Luther was sent to expound the doctrine of
nonviolence and forgiveness in the third quarter of the twentieth century. If Jesus was called to preach the Gospel to the
poor, Martin Luther was called to give dignity to the common man. If a prophet is one who interprets in clear and
intelligible language the will of God, Martin Luther King,
Jr. fits that designation. If a prophet is one who does not seek
popular causes to espouse, but rather the causes he thinks
are right, Martin Luther qualified on that score.

No! He was not ahead of his time. No man is ahead of
his time. Every man is within his star, each in his time. Each
man must respond to the call of God in his lifetime and not
in somebody else's time. Jesus had to respond to the call of
God in the first century A.D., and not in the twentieth century. He had but one life to live. He couldn't wait. How
long do you think Jesus would have had to wait for the constituted authorities to accept him? Twenty-five years? A hundred years? A thousand? He died at thirty-three. He couldn't
wait. Paul, Galileo, Copernicus, Martin Luther the Protestant reformer, Gandhi and Nehru couldn't wait for another
time. They had to act in their lifetimes. No man is ahead of
his time. Abraham, leaving his country in obedience to God's
call; Moses leading a rebellious people to the Promised
Land; Jesus dying on a cross; Galileo on his knees recanting;
Lincoln dying of an assassin's bullet; Woodrow Wilson cru-
sading for a League of Nations; Martin Luther King, Jr.
dying fighting for justice for garbage collectors—none of
these men were ahead of their time. With them the time was
always ripe to do that which was right and that which needed
to be done.

Too bad, you say, that Martin Luther King, Jr. died so young. I feel that way, too. But, as I have said many times before, it isn't how long one lives, but how well. It's what one accomplishes for mankind that matters. Jesus died at thirty-three; Joan of Arc at nineteen; Byron and Burns at thirty-six; Keats at twenty-five; Marlowe at twenty-nine; Shelley at thirty; Dunbar before thirty-five; John Fitzgerald Kennedy at forty-six; William Rainey Harper at forty-nine; and Martin Luther King, Jr. at thirty-nine.

We all pray that the assassin will be apprehended and brought to justice. But, make no mistake, the American people are in part responsible for Martin Luther King, Jr.'s death. The assassin heard enough condemnation of King and of Negroes to feel that he had public support. He knew that millions hated King.

The Memphis officials must bear some of the guilt for Martin Luther's assassination. The strike should have been settled several weeks ago. The lowest paid men in our society should not have to strike for a more just wage. A century after Emancipation, and after the enactment of the Thirteenth, Fourteenth, and Fifteenth Amendments, it should not have been necessary for Martin Luther King, Jr. to stage marches in Montgomery, Birmingham, and Selma, and go to jail thirty times trying to achieve for his people those rights which people of lighter hue get by virtue of their being born white. We, too, are guilty of murder. It is time for the American people to repent and make democracy equally applicable to all Americans. What can we do? *We,* and not the assassin, represent America at its best. *We* have the power— not the prejudiced, not the assassin—to make things right.

If we love Martin Luther King, Jr., and respect him, as this crowd surely testifies, let us see to it that he did not die in vain; let us see to it that we do not dishonor his name by trying to solve our problems through rioting in the streets. Violence was foreign to his nature. He warned that continued riots could produce a Fascist state. But let us see to it also that the conditions that cause riots are promptly removed, as the President of the United States is trying to get us to do. Let black and white alike search their hearts; and if there be prejudice in our hearts against any racial or ethnic group, let us exterminate it and let us pray, as Martin Luther King, Jr. would pray if he could: "Father, forgive them for they know not what they do." If we do this, Martin Luther King, Jr. will have died a redemptive death from which all mankind will benefit.

Morehouse College will never be the same because Martin Luther came by here; and the nation and the world will be indebted to him for centuries to come. It is natural, therefore, that we here at Morehouse and President Gloster would want to memorialize him to serve as an inspiration to all students who study in this Center.

I close by saying to you what Martin Luther King, Jr. believed: If physical death was the price he had to pay to rid America of prejudice and injustice, nothing could be more redemptive. And, to paraphrase the words of the immortal John Fitzgerald Kennedy, permit me to say that Martin Luther King, Jr.'s unfinished work on earth must truly be our own.

MEMORIAL CONVOCATION ADDRESS [3]

BUELL G. GALLAGHER [4]

"There are moments in the life of a nation when grief and outrage strike its people dumb, when words will not come because no words can express the agony in the nation's soul." So spoke Edward W. Brooke to his colleagues in the United States Senate on April 5, 1968—the day following the assassination of Dr. Martin Luther King, Jr. A victim of the violence which he abhorred, Dr. King symbolized what is good and true and just in the great American dream. With unremitting fervor and olympian patience, he strove to cleanse the nation of the manifold ills arising from racial discrimination. Using the Ghandian methods of nonviolent political action, he doubtless did more than any man of this generation to lay bare the racial ills of the land, and to point out the remedies available to men of good and peaceful intent.

The eloquence of Dr. King has now been stilled. But surely the vision of a better land, so dramatically sealed in his "I Have a Dream," will guide us yet to the proud estate of freedom and equality for all.

Memorial convocations and services for Dr. King were held throughout the United States, as well as abroad. In an outpouring of concern and rededication unmatched since the death of President John F. Kennedy, the nation paid its final respects to the fallen martyr. Colleges and universities joined impressively in the solemn calls for expiation.

On April 8, 1968, the City College of New York held its ceremony in Dr. King's honor. With some 1400 students and faculty members in attendance in the Great Hall, and with additional hundreds hearing the service over loudspeakers set up at other stations at the College, President Buell G. Gallagher pronounced the Invocation and delivered the memorial address. Dr. Gallagher's statement is an eloquent tribute to a man whom he knew well and to a cause with which he has himself been importantly associated during a long professional career.

[3] The Great Hall, City College of the City University of New York, April 8, 1968. Text furnished by Dr. Gallagher and I. E. Levine, Director of Public Relations, with permission for this reprint.

[4] For biographical note, see Appendix.

The invocation:

Look upon us, O Lord, folk of many families and races, gathered together beneath the peace of this roof in solemn and bewildered mourning for the death of Thy servant, Martin Luther King. Be Thou with us, to comfort our affliction in this hour of great need. Take not from us the meaning of this hour, even as we are solaced; but so strengthen our resolution and cement our commitment that from this tragedy we may take new strength, new dedication, new hope.

Amen.

When Martin Luther King strode into the Lewisohn Stadium to address the graduating classes, it was only two days after the assassination of Medgar Evers. All through the dinner which preceded the Commencement Exercises, he had been more than usually solemn and subdued. And that mood carried with him as he spoke in restrained phrase the winged words of the address.

Because he knew, as we knew, that the life of reason is under constant threat from unreasoning violence. He knew, as we knew, that the affirmation of love is always challenged by the merchants of hatred. He knew, as we knew, that the assassination of Medgar Evers was only the most recent in a continuing series of reminders that the angel of death always hovers near the agents of peace.

Early in his career he had committed himself to an unremitting nonviolent struggle for equality, justice and brotherhood. But even as he made his commitment to nonviolence, he knew that others might respond with violence. Gandhi himself had been cut down by an assassin. In a world of violence, no prophet of peace could claim immunity. And at thirty-nine, steadfastly refusing to abandon the path on which, at twenty-five, he had set his feet, he gave his life.

He was a dedicated man. And from the depths of his spirit there welled up words which gave eloquence to profound conviction and commitment. In Montgomery he found the answer to bus segregation in the boycott when he said, "We will walk . . . with God!" The rightness of his determination would later be affirmed by the Supreme Court. On the road to Selma, he answered those who urged the abandoning of nonviolence when he shouted, "Don't ask me to descend to the level of those who use violence!" Retribution, he declared, is not the answer: not retribution—redemption. And he meant what he said. He was true to his faith till death. Whether his death will, indeed, prove to be redemptive is now for others to decide.

This nation, this city, this college, each one of us and all of us together have one final moment of decision still open.

We have had many previous warnings. As the lynchings of earlier decades were supplanted by selected assassination, we watched with dismay and anger. As organized hatred became resurgent, we watched with dismay and apprehension. When an NAACP worker was killed in Mississippi, and four little girls were crushed in the bombing of a Birmingham church, and three young civil rights workers were buried beneath an earthen dam, and Malcolm X was brutally slaughtered by conspiracy—each time, we had another warning. In the hot summer of Watts, when a whole community for the first time blatantly rejected the nonviolent leadership of Martin Luther King, drowning his eloquence in angry shouts for revenge, we had the most foreboding warning of all. But we did not hear. In the agony of the inner city in Newark and Detroit and a score of cities—from Los Angeles to Boston and from Chicago to Jacksonville, from Lenox Avenue and Beale Street, the rising surge of frustration and anger has drowned the voices of hope and replaced faith with doubt in the hearts of many. There are those who say that since we failed to respond to all these other warnings, it is clear that we will fail once again. They say that this latest act of senseless brutality in Memphis has driven us over the brink into national insanity from which there is no recovery.

I disagree, as Martin Luther King would have disagreed.

I dare to believe that the tombs of the prophets are the ramparts of civilization, that the blood of the martyrs is the seed of the church, that the death of this great and good man will be redemptive.

I am sick and tired of all this killing and hatred. I am sick and tired of racism—white or black or yellow or pink. I am sick and tired of war, whether in Vietnam or on H Street in Washington or in Bedford Stuyvesant or on Convent Avenue. I am sick and tired of the class war and of the poverty from which it stems. I am sick and tired of snobbery and cynicism among the intellectual elite and of bitterness and despair among the dispossessed. I am sick and tired of anything which sets man against his brother.

But beyond this sickness and weariness there beckons a great hope toward which I move with consuming passion and absolute dedication.

I see this nation finding its way through to the day when the only American presence on foreign soil will be unarmed. I see our streets safe for the aged and the infirm; our parks happy with children playing—together; our homes purchased or occupied without reference to the accident of birth and heritage; our schools thronged with children who learn well because teachers no longer doubt that they *can* learn; public office no longer conditioned upon religious or racial background; the City College campus happy with youth and adults of every race, religion and class who hold each the other in mutual respect and warm affection and who are intolerant only of intolerance—an integrated college, as an integral part of an integrated city; the end of violence and hatred and the building of the Beloved Community.

Do not tell me that this is an idle dream! Come up to the mountain. Stand there with the living memory of Martin Luther King. He knew that dreams are never idle—that only *men* are idle, when unmoved by dreams.

Preaching in Atlanta last February, he said that all he wanted to leave behind as his legacy was "a committed life." Well, he has done his part. That legacy will now be claimed only by those who commit themselves to the nonviolent achievement of an open society redeemed by self-sacrifice. He died for the Beloved Community. Surely it is not asking too much of others, that they live for it.

On the Georgia coast there is a place known as Ebo's Landing. Tradition has it that it is so named because of an incident involving the Ebo [Ibo] tribe.

A slave runner had landed under cover of darkness to discharge his illicit cargo. During the night the intended slaves, all members of the Ebo tribe, continued in council— and reached their decision. With the dawn, they joined hands and walked down to the beach. Men, women and children, they waded out to greet the rising sun—singing—to their death, preferring that to slavery. They were free.

So it is today, that from the full throats of two score millions of Americans the ancient spiritual rises, beating on the ears of white America with a new—and final—insistence. But one word is changed. Now we hear, "Let my people *come!*"

Let us pray:

We remember, O Lord, the committed life and labor of Thy servant, Martin Luther King, and commit our lives and labors to the building of his dream.

Do Thou, O God, comfort and sustain his family and this nation in our hour of grief.

Support us all the day long of this mortal life, until the evening shadows lengthen, the busy world is hushed, life's fever is over, and our work is done. And then in Thy great mercy grant us a safe lodging, a holy rest, and peace at the last. Amen.

A TRIBUTE TO SENATOR ROBERT F. KENNEDY [5]

EDWARD M. KENNEDY [6]

"It is not his death but his life that speaks volumes against the folly and futility of violence." So wrote Theodore C. Sorensen in his memoir of Senator Robert F. Kennedy, who died on June 6, 1968, from gunshot wounds. Within a period of sixty days, two distinguished Americans fell before the assassins' bullets. And the nation searched its individual and collective conscience for an answer, however imperfect, to the paradox of violence directed against its men of peace and honor.

In a statement reminiscent of Robert G. Ingersoll's speech of June 3, 1879, at his brother's grave, Senator Edward M. Kennedy paid final tribute to his brother at the requiem mass on June 8, 1968, at St. Patrick's Cathedral in New York City. Some 2,300 people, including President Johnson, attended the solemn rites. In addition, an estimated 150 million Americans witnessed some parts of the services over the three major television networks.

In this moment of profound grief, the only remaining Kennedy brother could yet speak of national rededication and of hope for a better world. "My brother," he said, "saw wrong and tried to right it, saw suffering and tried to heal it, saw war and tried to stop it. Those of us who loved him and who take him to his rest today, pray that what he was to us and what he wished for others will some day come to pass for all the world."

Like Martin Luther King, Jr., Robert F. Kennedy had a dream. What a shocking commentary on the quality of our culture that neither was permitted a view of the new horizon that each envisioned.

On behalf of Mrs. Robert Kennedy, her children and the parents and sisters of Robert Kennedy, I want to express what we feel to those who mourn with us today in this cathedral and around the world. We loved him as a brother and father and son. From his parents, and from his older brothers and sisters—Joe, Kathleen and Jack—he received inspira-

[5] St. Patrick's Cathedral, New York City, June 8, 1968. Text furnished by Richard C. Drayne, Press Aide to Senator Edward M. Kennedy, with permission for this reprint.

[6] For biographical note, see Appendix.

tion which he passed on to all of us. He gave us strength in time of trouble, wisdom in time of uncertainty, and sharing in time of happiness. He was always by our side.

Love is not an easy feeling to put into words. Nor is loyalty, or trust or joy. But he was all of these. He loved life completely and lived it intensely.

A few years back, Robert Kennedy wrote some words about his own father and they expressed the way we in his family feel about him. He said of what his father meant to him: "What it really all adds up to is love—not love as it is described with such facility in popular magazines, but the kind of love that is affection and respect, order, encouragement, and support. Our awareness of this was an incalculable source of strength, and because real love is something unselfish and involves sacrifice and giving, we could not help but profit from it.

"Beneath it all, he has tried to engender a social conscience. There were wrongs which needed attention. There were people who were poor and who needed help. And we have a responsibility to them and to this country. Through no virtues and accomplishments of our own, we have been fortunate enough to be born in the United States under the most comfortable conditions. We, therefore, have a responsibility to others who are less well off."

This is what Robert Kennedy was given. What he leaves us is what he said, what he did and what he stood for. A speech he made to the young people of South Africa on their Day of Affirmation in 1966 sums it up the best, and I would read it now:

"There is discrimination in this world and slavery and slaughter and starvation. Governments repress their people; and millions are trapped in poverty while the nation grows rich; and wealth is lavished on armaments everywhere.

"These are differing evils, but they are common works of man. They reflect the imperfection of human justice, the inadequacy of human compassion, our lack of sensibility toward the sufferings of our fellows.

"But we can perhaps remember—even if only for a time—that those who live with us are our brothers; that they share with us the same short moment of life; that they seek—as we do—nothing but the chance to live out their lives in purpose and happiness, winning what satisfaction and fulfillment they can.

"Surely this bond of common faith, this bond of common goal, can begin to teach us something. Surely, we can learn, at least, to look at those around us as fellow men. And surely we can begin to work a little harder to bind up the wounds among us and to become in our own hearts brothers and countrymen once again.

"Our answer is to rely on youth—not a time of life but a state of mind, a temper of the will, a quality of imagination, a predominance of courage over timidity, of the appetite for adventure over the love of ease. The cruelties and obstacles of this swiftly changing planet will not yield to obsolete dogmas and outworn slogans. They cannot be moved by those who cling to a present that is already dying, who prefer the illusion of security to the excitement and danger that come with even the most peaceful progress. It is a revolutionary world we live in; and this generation, at home and around the world, has had thrust upon it a greater burden of responsibility than any generation that has ever lived.

"Some believe there is nothing one man or one woman can do against the enormous array of the world's ills. Yet many of the world's great movements, of thought and action, have flowed from the work of a single man. A young monk began the Protestant reformation, a young general extended an empire from Macedonia to the borders of the earth, and a young woman reclaimed the territory of France. It was a young Italian explorer who discovered the New World, and the thirty-two-year-old Thomas Jefferson who proclaimed that all men are created equal.

"These men moved the world, and so can we all. Few will have the greatness to bend history itself, but each of us can work to change a small portion of events, and in the total of all those acts will be written the history of this generation. It is from numberless diverse acts of courage and belief that human history is shaped. Each time a man stands up for an ideal, or acts to improve the lot of others, or strikes out against injustice, he sends forth a tiny ripple of hope, and crossing each other from a million different centers of energy and daring, those ripples build a current that can sweep down the mightiest walls of oppression and resistance.

"Few are willing to brave the disapproval of their fellows, the censure of their colleagues, the wrath of their society. Moral courage is a rarer commodity than bravery in battle or great intelligence. Yet it is the one essential, vital quality for those who seek to change a world that yields most painfully to change. And I believe that in this generation those with the courage to enter the moral conflict will find themselves with companions in every corner of the globe.

"For the fortunate among us, there is the temptation to follow the easy and familiar paths of personal ambition and financial success so grandly spread before those who enjoy the privilege of education. But that is not the road history has marked out for us. Like it or not, we live in times of danger and uncertainty. But they are also more open to the creative energy of men than any other time in history. All of us will ultimately be judged and as the years pass we will surely judge ourselves, on the effort we have contributed to building a new world society and the extent to which our ideals and goals have shaped that effort.

"The future does not belong to those who are content with today, apathetic toward common problems and their fellow man alike, timid and fearful in the face of new ideas and bold projects. Rather it will belong to those who can blend vision, reason and courage in a personal commitment to the ideals and great enterprises of American society.

"Our future may lie beyond our vision, but it is not completely beyond our control. It is the shaping impulse of America that neither fate nor nature nor the irresistible tides of history, but the work of our own hands, matched to reason and principle, that will determine our destiny. There is pride in that, even arrogance, but there is also experience and truth. In any event, it is the only way we can live."

This is the way he lived. My brother need not be idealized, or enlarged in death beyond what he was in life, to be remembered simply as a good and decent man, who saw wrong and tried to right it, saw suffering and tried to heal it, saw war and tried to stop it.

Those of us who loved him and who take him to his rest today, pray that what he was to us and what he wished for others will some day come to pass for all the world.

As he said many times, in many parts of this nation, to those he touched and who sought to touch him:

"Some men see things as they are and say why.

I dream things that never were and say why not."

OF EARTH AND SKY

WHY FOREIGN AID? [1]

WILLIAM S. GAUD [2]

Admittedly, it is difficult to trace the long-range effects of a speech. Over the years, however, ideas set forth in certain addresses continue to exercise such pervasive influence upon public and private action that none but the most confirmed skeptics could doubt that the speeches had consequences. Surely Abraham Lincoln's "Cooper Institute Address" mattered; as did some of Franklin D. Roosevelt's fireside chats, Ralph Waldo Emerson's "The American Scholar," and the Kennedy-Nixon debates of 1960. But for the Vietnam war, President Johnson's "Great Society" speech at Ann Arbor, Michigan, on May 22, 1964, might have achieved a more durable status.

Doubtless a prime example of continuing rhetorical influence is Secretary of State General George C. Marshall's speech at Harvard University on June 5, 1947. The substance of the speech derived from a series of reflections and actions by high government officials. President Truman's speech of March 12, 1947, set forth a "doctrine of containment" of Soviet expansion and a prospect of aid to Turkey and Greece. In a little-known speech at Cleveland, Mississippi, in early May 1947, Under Secretary of State Dean Acheson spoke of the need for an imaginative program which would hasten the economic recovery of Europe. George F. Kennan, National War College Deputy for Foreign Affairs, had been asked by General Marshall to initiate a Policy Planning Staff in the United States Department of State which would address itself to the urgent problems of European recovery. On May 23, the recommendations were turned over to Marshall. Passages from the report, according to Mr. Kennan, appeared a few days later in Mr. Marshall's speech at Harvard. At the Paris Conference in July 1947, the European Economic Recovery Plan came into existence. At any rate, Mr. Marshall's ad-

[1] Economic Club of Detroit, Detroit, Michigan, December 4, 1967. Text furnished by E. A. Comee, Chief of the Public Affairs Division, Information Staff, United States Department of State, Agency for International Development, with permission for this reprint.

[2] For biographical note, see Appendix.

dress at Harvard gave a kind of official stamp to a variety of previous pronouncements.

By any reasonable standard, the economic program must be adjudged a success. In fact, many of the European countries formerly receiving substantial assistance from the United States are themselves now directing sizable sums to help underdeveloped lands in South America, Asia, and Africa.

The term Marshall Plan has come to be associated with any major undertaking requiring massive human effort and public financing. Currently, such a plan for urban salvation is mentioned by high officials, including Vice President Hubert H. Humphrey and Whitney Young of the National Urban League. And there have been similar proposals for a Marshall Plan for the humanities and arts.

The enormously extensive aid programs, plus the mutual security expenditures, have over the past twenty years provoked unending debate, some of it not unmixed with rancor. The recommended appropriations—for agricultural development, or education, or population control—have in some quarters met with unceasing opposition. But in the end the cause has prevailed, not always as heartily as its supporters would hope—but it has prevailed.

Strong leaders with deep convictions have fought hard for the aid program. Chief among the present advocates of continuing aid is William S. Gaud, Jr., since 1966 the Administrator of the Agency for International Development. A forthright man, Mr. Gaud presents concise, articulate defenses of foreign aid and tries to correct skeptical impressions of the programs arising from misinformation.

The speech reprinted below was given before the Economic Club of Detroit on December 4, 1967. In it, Mr. Gaud indicated why the developing nations need assistance, and why they do not have time to develop slowly, as did, indeed, the United States with some help from England, France, and other European countries. He devoted his talk to two propositions, providing an abundance of illustrative material in support of both: (1) development aid works, and (2) it is in our national interest to provide assistance. He concluded by saying that our choice today and for some years to come is clear: "It lies between investing in international stability and surrendering to the frustrations of living in a difficult and imperfect world."

It is a pleasure to be in Detroit and to be with the Economic Club. This city has contributed a great deal to the economic and social development of the United States. And this forum has a national reputation for attracting and involving the leaders of Detroit. It is a privilege to appear before you.

I propose to talk to you today not about foreign aid in general, nor about military assistance, but about that part of our foreign aid program which is designed to promote economic and social development in the emerging nations. And let me make no bones about it: I want to enlist your active support for this part of our program. Foreign aid today badly needs domestic help.

Twenty years ago, the then senior Senator from Michigan, Arthur Vandenberg, led the bipartisan effort for adoption of the Marshall Plan. Senator Vandenberg said it was in "the clear self-interest of the United States" to help in the rebuilding of Europe.

The Marshall Plan put economic starch into our commitment to European security. It represented, in effect, a peacetime extension of our wartime alliance. Everyone will agree, I am sure, that it was both very much in our interest and highly successful.

Today, the Old World no longer needs our aid. But as President Eisenhower put it in 1957, "new forces and new nations stir and strive across the earth, with power to bring . . . great good or great evil to the free world. . . ." These nations do need our aid. President Eisenhower declared in this same speech that "one third of all mankind" was in need of "at least a spark of hope, the hope of progress." That is still true.

Today, there is a real possibility that this hope for progress will not be realized. The Decade of Development is in danger of becoming the Decade of Disappointment.

The Congress has not yet passed a foreign aid appropriation bill for the fiscal year which began last July 1. It will probably do so within the next week or ten days. When it does, there is every likelihood that it will be the smallest aid bill ever. In the opinion of the President, in the opinion of

the Secretary of State and in my own opinion it will be too
small to serve our interests adequately. For example:

We will have to reduce sharply our programs in India,
in Pakistan and in Africa.

We will not be able to carry out our part of the plans
made last spring at the Punta del Este Conference to
increase efforts in agriculture, education, and health
under the Alliance for Progress.

We will have to shortchange our security-oriented and
military aid programs in East Asia and elsewhere.

This decline in the fortunes of foreign aid is not a phenomenon which has come upon us overnight. President George
Woods of the World Bank has repeatedly stated that the
needs of the developing world for outside assistance are not
being met. Yet, while our gross national product has increased nearly 150 per cent over the past fifteen years, the
share of our gross national product which we are devoting to
foreign aid has shrunk by roughly 50 per cent. In short, as we
have been able to afford more, we have done less.

There is a tendency to blame the difficulties of foreign
aid on the Congress. Or, if one looks beyond the Congress,
to blame them on Vietnam, summer violence in our cities,
the budget deficit, the tax bill or our balance of payments
situation.

These are easy explanations, but I think the real explanation lies elsewhere. In my view, it lies with the American
people. Too few Americans understand the purposes of the
foreign aid program and how it serves their interests. Too
many are asking: What has this got to do with us? How does
this help the United States? Why should we have foreign aid?

Misinformation about foreign aid may be partly responsible for this confusion and uncertainty. Some misinformation
about a program as varied and as complex as this is inevitable. But I feel that our primary problem arises from a lack
of understanding of two very simple and very basic propositions. First, development aid does work. Second, it is not a

woolly-headed giveaway. It is a program which definitely and concretely serves our interests.

It is these two propositions which I want to talk about today.

First, however, let me say a few words as to why the developing nations need help.

The development of our own country took many years. It was supported by considerable outside capital and investment. It was our good fortune that England, Germany, the Netherlands and other European powers invested heavily in this country.

Loans were made first to state and local governments; later, increasingly, to private industry. Shortly after 1800, we had foreign obligations of $75 million. By 1843 the total was $225 million. At the start of this century, it was $3.3 billion.

British capital helped develop our railroads. The Erie and Ohio Canals were both financed in considerable part with European money.

Until the turn of the present century our development proceeded at a relatively slow pace. We had time to develop slowly. Nothing in the world moved as fast then as it does today. The world was larger, less interdependent; the expectations of both men and nations were more modest; and they were more patient about realizing them. The United States could afford to wait for its foreign exchange earnings to increase to the point where they could finance loans from abroad. We were under no pressure to move faster.

None of this is true of today's world. The emerging nations of the twentieth century are under pressure to grow at a much faster rate than that at which we grew in the eighteenth and nineteenth centuries.

One source of this new pressure is internal. It comes from surging birth rates. When Europe and this country were developing we desperately needed people to operate new industries and to expand markets for agriculture and manufacturing. Population growth stimulated progress. Today, in the backward countries, high birth rates hobble development. In many, agriculture is inadequate to feed their people. And there is not enough industry to employ them. Scarce resources must be used for food aid and to modernize agriculture.

In the United States and Europe, development preceded population growth. In today's developing world, the sequence has been reversed. This change in timing is an unlucky fact of history. The modern world has no choice but to cope with it.

Demand for progress in the new nations also arises from outside factors. The people of the less-developed nations now know what goes on in the developed world. Communities which have stood still for centuries are determined to change. Backward, pastoral ways are no longer tolerated. More and more of the governments of the new nations feel this pressure. More and more of them are responding with development programs.

In sum, the developing world is no longer content with inadequate diets, illiteracy, disease, and lack of opportunity. They want to change, and they want and need to change fast.

Now for the first of my two propositions—namely, that development aid can and does work.

What is development aid? It consists primarily of two things: development loans and technical assistance. Development loans are dollar loans made on concessionary terms to nations with inadequate foreign exchange resources. They are made for specific purposes: to cover the costs of specific projects, or to cover the imports of specific commodities and raw materials. They must be spent in the United States. Indeed better than 88 per cent of all foreign aid funds spent by the Agency for International Development are spent in the United States for U.S. goods, products and services.

Technical assistance is the present-day equivalent of President Truman's Point IV program. Its purpose is to help the developing nations acquire the trained manpower and institutions they need to develop their economies, achieve necessary social reforms and build viable social and political institutions. We rely heavily upon American universities, co-operatives, savings and loan institutions and labor unions and on other private concerns to carry out these technical assistance programs.

Last week we celebrated the end of our program of economic aid to Iran. From now on, Iran will look to its own resources—and to conventional lending sources—to finance its further growth.

There is a temptation to explain this success with one word—oil. And it is true that Iran is lucky in its geology. Oil revenues have been essential to Iran's progress. But the important thing has been the use Iran had made of its oil revenue. Three fourths of it has been applied to development—much of it to the land reform which the Shah calls the "white revolution" to distinguish it from "red" revolutions in other countries. Between 1952 and 1966, nearly $3 billion in Iranian funds went into development—about five times the total of United States economic aid.

But money by itself—no matter where it comes from—will not alone do the job of development. Development involves painful choices—sacrifices. It takes courage and toughness to exact them—leaders with a sure sense of direction, with the will and political strength to make development policies stick. It also takes people who are willing to respond to such leadership. All of these Iran has had. The Shah and his people have proven their commitment to the task of development.

Iran is agricultural. Nearly four fifths of its people are rural. Farming accounts for almost one third of the gross national product. The country's effort has focused on agriculture. Nearly one quarter of the funds spent under the current development plan have been used to bring additional land into production; to assist farmers in buying fertilizer, pesticides and equipment; and for irrigation, electrification and community development.

Most important, land that used to be closely held is now widely distributed. A new class of small-farm owners has emerged. Their interest in the land is a vital incentive. As would be expected, their output has jumped: rice, sugar, tea and cotton crops have all doubled in the past ten years. At the same time their purchasing power has gone up. The "white revolution" has given 14 million Iranians a direct stake in agricultural progress and thereby engaged them in the national effort to develop their nation.

Industry has also grown. Production is up 88 per cent over 1956—exports by more than a third. The gross national product has increased by $1.8 billion since 1962.

Development has worked in Iran because of Iran's own efforts. We helped—yes—by supporting the government and its programs when help was needed most. Since 1952 our aid to Iran—part of it in loans and part of it in grants—has totaled $605 million. Significantly, only $37 million of this—roughly 6 per cent—was extended in the last five years. In short, Iran's reliance on outside assistance has been decreasing steadily for a number of years. Iran has now reached the end of economic aid, or the beginning of self-sufficiency. Put it either way you like. To the United States and to other developed nations, this also means that Iran now offers important opportunities both for investment and for export trade.

Iran is not the only country where we have concluded development aid. Taiwan and Greece are two more. And steady, substantial progress is being made in a number of other countries where the necessary will and resources are at work.

In Korea in the late 1950's and early 1960's, aid did little more than keep the Korean economy barely afloat. A raging inflation, shortsighted fiscal, monetary and economic policies and ineffective leadership all but dissipated our help.

Then, in the early 1960's a new government with pride and a sense of nationhood set out to stabilize the Korean economy. Tight ceilings limited credit, government deficits, the use of foreign exchange, and the incurring of foreign commercial debt. United States aid was conditioned on the performance of these and other stabilization and reform measures.

It worked. Inflation abated. Investment became attractive. Domestic savings—vital to development—began to grow. Manufacturing flourished. Exports jumped—from $20 to $30 million yearly in the 1950's to $250 million last year. Today, American and other foreign investors are being attracted to Korea. Korea is on its way. Internal leadership and drive, complemented by outside assistance, are making a success of Korea's development program.

Many factors go to make up a successful development effort. Few, in my view, are more significant than an active, growing, driving private sector.

In some underdeveloped countries there has been ideological resistance to giving the private sector its head. In some, private enterprise is linked with colonialism or imperialism.

But in recent years, as the leaders of developing nations have had to face up to the tough problems of raising production and organizing regional and national economies, more and more of them have come to realize the importance of private initiative and private enterprise. Today, most of the nations high on the growth lists display vigorous and growing private sectors.

On Taiwan, remarkable growth has directly paralleled the change in the economy from one mainly controlled by government, to one that consists mostly of private enterprise. In India, in the past, there was considerable doctrinaire hostility to private enterprise. Today, an industry key to Indian progress—fertilizer production—has been opened up to private enterprise. In Colombia, Korea, Mexico, Pakistan, Thailand and other countries where economies are moving ahead, much of the push comes from the private sector.

We are convinced that no country can develop except through its own efforts, through what we call self-help. The question thus arises of what we can do to induce or persuade a country to take the self-help measures that will move it along the path of progress. We use our influence to promote sound development policies and the sensible use of a country's own resources. In fact, however, only one sixth of all investment in the developing countries comes from the outside. The rest is self-financed.

Our contribution to any one country's development effort is relatively small, and thus our influence—or leverage—is limited. Nevertheless, we can and do link development aid with specific economic policies, administrative measures and social reforms.

This process works. Indeed, it often works because the very self-help measures we are supporting need outside financial support if they are to succeed.

For example, in Pakistan several years ago, shortages of foreign exchange meant that industrial raw materials were chronically scarce. As a result, manufacturing plants were underused, production was low, prices high. In 1964, after much encouragement from us, the Pakistan government lifted import controls. They did this with our assurance that we would provide a large part of our assistance in the form of scarce industrial commodities and raw materials. Thus, supplies of key materials would increase without draining away precious foreign exchange. The controls went off, supplies increased, production went up and prices went down. Pakistan market forces and free enterprise got more play. Outside aid both encouraged and made possible the specific policy reform we had been urging.

The developing world does not consist exclusively of Pakistans and Koreas. Not all the new nations have the trained manpower and institutions to make good use of development aid. Not all can mobilize enough capital of their own to carry out a development program. Not all have the political strength to insist on unpopular self-help measures. And not all are sophisticated enough to handle relations with aid donors who make policy reforms a condition of aid.

This shortage of qualified candidates for development explains why our development aid is concentrated in only a few countries. In the current fiscal year, about four fifths of AID's [Agency for International Development] development loans will go to just seven countries: Brazil, Chile, Colombia, India, Korea, Pakistan, and Turkey.

We do, as you know, have aid programs in many more countries than these. Some of them, such as our programs in Vietnam, the Dominican Republic, and the Congo, are security oriented. They have their roots in political considerations. Others are in countries which have not yet progressed enough to support a broad development program. In these countries our programs are modest in size. They consist primarily of technical assistance, chiefly in the fields of agriculture, education and health. Here, our interest is in training individuals, creating institutions and building infrastructure against the day when these new nations can undertake more ambitious development programs.

But almost all of the dozen or so countries which have been receiving large amounts of development assistance over the past several years have made appreciable progress. Their growth rates are high. Their ability to sustain these rates is substantial and improving. About half the group have considerably reduced their dependence on outside assistance. A few, as I have mentioned, have dispensed with concessional aid altogether.

All in all, this is an impressive record of performance. Development aid *can* work. It is working now in many parts of this restless world.

Now for my second proposition: That it is in our national interest to carry on a foreign aid program aimed at development.

Our interests in the world, as well as the objectives of our aid program, have changed greatly since the days of the Marshall Plan—and also since the early days of the cold war when our aid program was preponderantly security-oriented and extended military assistance. Many people fail to recognize these differences. They judge the new by the standards of the old. As a result, they often expect the wrong things from today's aid program and are dissatisfied when their expectations are not realized.

The earlier programs which helped to rebuild Europe—and which built up the defenses of Greece, Turkey, Taiwan and Korea—had deep fears behind them. Fear for the future of the Western Alliance, fear of Communist aggression, fear that the cold war would go against us. The Western Alliance was designed to contain the causes of our fear. The aid programs which supported that alliance clearly served the national interest. The connection between our assistance program and our interests abroad was crystal clear.

Today, many of the fears of the early cold war have waned, and the tie between our foreign aid and our foreign policy is more complex.

There is a second key difference between foreign aid twenty years ago and today. It is in our relations with the nations which receive our assistance. In the aftermath of the war, much of our aid program was an extension of wartime relations with intimate allies. Aid went largely to old friends —to nations with whom Americans felt strong common bonds. In 1948, when Senator Vandenberg introduced the European Recovery Program in the Senate, he pointed out that Europe was "the stock which has largely made America." As he put it, the Marshall Plan was essential because "Western civilization" depended on European independence.

Today, outside Latin America, the nations receiving development aid from the United States are not, by and large, this country's old friends. They are our new neighbors. Many are new to nationhood. They have emerged from the wave of decolonization which, since the war, has more than doubled the number of sovereign states. In the past, most of their people had little to do with the United States. Our present relations with them lack the historical ties and political and military intimacy that supported the Western alliance after the war. In short, where fear for our security helped to motivate aid we are now less afraid. Where we gave aid to old friends, we now help new nations. Where aid supported key alliances, it is now extended outside the old defense framework.

These differences are grounded in changes in the world—and in changes in our interests in the world. The focus of United States foreign policy has widened since the years immediately following World War II. The challenges to that policy have also changed. But today's challenges are no less real, no less compelling than the challenge of fifteen and twenty years ago.

The dominant interest of the nations of more than half the free world has switched in recent years—from traditional political goals to development. National progress now overshadows all other goals in the less developed world. This drive for national progress has become a paramount fact of world affairs. Nothing is more characteristic of the world today—nothing will do more to shape the world tomorrow—than the determination of the new nations to realize goals which are still far beyond their reach.

How can a strong program to assist development serve our national interests in today's world?

First, let me say that Americans should disabuse themselves of the notion that the purpose of such a program is to win friends, earn gratitude or gain votes in the United Nations. Development aid is a poor tool for the attainment of any of these goals. Development aid serves our foreign policy in ways which go far beyond these.

The critical fact for our relations with the developing nations is that their new goals *are* beyond their reach. They cannot attain them alone. They need help, and they look to us and other developed nations to provide it.

To conduct meaningful relations with the backward half of the world, the United States must recognize the urgency of its need for progress. As a major power, we have the strength to force our way on issues that concern us. But political relations involve more than the threat of force; our own sensibilities tend to curb the use of force. So long as national progress is the overwhelming concern of the new nations, we must work with them to achieve their goals. Our aid programs offer a way to meet both our national interests in the world and the aspirations of the developing nations.

Foreign aid is also right. As citizens of the richest and most powerful nation on earth, it would be wrong for us to shrug our shoulders at the conditions in which the people of the developing countries now live.

Finally, development is necessary for the achievement of a stable peace. The underdeveloped nations are dependent and vulnerable; their weakness leads to instability in the world; their increased independence can help to keep the peace. Aid for development will not guarantee stability or peace. But when we neglect development, we invite instability and collisions between nations.

In neglecting development, we also encourage unrest, racism and hostility within the new nations. The target, inevitably, is the developed half of the world. When we neglect development, we jeopardize the possibility of peace.

To conclude: in half the world, there is tremendous and unprecedented pressure for development. There has never been anything like it. We do not have pat solutions to all the problems this pressure raises. Indeed, the main response must come from the emerging nations themselves. But we can play an important role, and we have already done so. We have made key contributions to development success in some countries, and we have promising work underway in many others. Development aid does work.

Development aid does not meet all the foreign policy objectives of the United States. Indeed, day to day, our assistance efforts can raise problems—while we are meeting problems that run from decade to decade.

But for the rest of this century, the phenomena of development will be a large part of the raw material of American foreign relations. This is certain. We must accept it. It means that foreign aid for development will be integral to our foreign policy, and essential to our interests.

Twenty years ago, when the United States ended the war, we did not enter the world in order to police it or to expand our influence, or even to play Santa Claus and give away our share. The new compactness of the world put us in the world and has kept us in it. There is no getting out. Our size and wealth endow us with a large role on this planet. We cannot hide from our own dimensions and power.

These, it seems to me, are facts of life—just as the drive for development is a fact of life. Are we now to ignore these facts, turn our backs on the world and tell other nations to solve their problems without our help? Could we do this even if we wished? Do we care about international stability, about peace, about the kind of world we will leave to our children?

These questions answer themselves. The choice is clear. It lies between investing in international stability and surrendering to the frustrations of living in a difficult and imperfect world.

I urge you to make your choice and—having made it—see that your counsel is heard.

FROM RUNNYMEDE TO GANYMEDE [3]

James E. Webb [4]

Slightly more than ten years ago, the Soviet Union success-fully launched its first Sputnik. The world has not been quite the same since. What a few decades ago seemed pure fantasy, imaginative dreaming, suddenly became fact, and fact with incred-ible social implication. Not only was man about to view and partially conquer the seemingly unattainable frontier of space; he was also about to open a competitive race in which science, sophis-ticated technology, and human survival play fatefully interlocked roles.

The civilian space program in the United States is doubtless the most complex technological venture on record. It is not only large; it is expensive, a multibillion-dollar undertaking. Needless to say, it is dramatic, as any TV viewer who has followed the re-ports of a manned space vehicle in orbit knows. Even in this, its infancy, the program has produced results which defy belief in the average citizen. What is to come soon may make the early triumphs look like elementary exercises. Completion of the Apollo moon project by 1970 is a possibility; a landing on Mars in the 1980's is not beyond reasonable prediction.

The scientific nerve center of this complex venture is the National Aeronautics and Space Administration. In effect a merger of several military and nonmilitary enterprises, NASA was or-ganized in 1958, with Dr. T. Keith Glennan as administrator. In 1961, President John F. Kennedy appointed James E. Webb as Glennan's successor, and virtually instructed him to put a man on the moon by 1970.

Highly skilled in administrative management, Mr. Webb brought to the post wide experience in government and business. Director of the Bureau of the Budget under President Truman and later Under Secretary of State, Mr. Webb subsequently served as president of the Republic Supply Company and took part in a variety of business ventures in the manufacture of aircraft and oil equipment. This background has served him well in main-

[3] Prelude to Independence Celebration, Williamsburg, Virginia, May 27, 1967. Text furnished by Colonial Williamsburg. Permission to reprint granted by Colonial Williamsburg and Julian Scheer, Assistant Administrator for Public Affairs, National Aeronautics and Space Administration.

[4] For biographical note, see Appendix.

taining a delicate balance among research institutions, the aerospace industry, and NASA—all of which contribute importantly to the far-flung technological operation which a missile expert called "a science Olympics in which you're supposed to do the 100-yard dash in three seconds."

Since 1966, when its expenditures were near the $6 billion mark, the space program has lost some of its thrust. The Apollo project has run into technical difficulties; employment in the space industry has slackened; and the public has offered some resistance to space ventures while troubles here on earth plague the nation so grievously.

Mr. Webb is a vigorous exponent of the space mission. He speaks often before college and community audiences, and always with great enthusiasm and at an uninterruptedly fast rate. His rapid-fire delivery prompted a NASA official to remark that "trying to make conversation with Jim Webb is like trying to drink out of a fire hydrant." Said John Mecklin in a *Fortune* article: "Most people react initially to Webb with bewilderment, but then find themselves captivated by his intensity."

On May 27, 1967, Mr. Webb delivered the annual address at the eighteenth-century colonial capitol in Williamsburg, Virginia, on the occasion of the celebration of the Prelude to Independence. This is an impressive event which in recent years has enlisted such distinguished speakers as Glenn Seaborg, Arnold J. Toynbee, Sir Patrick Dean, Charles Malik, and Barbara Ward. The ceremony memorializes the period from May 15 through July 4, 1776, during which three important actions were taken by the Virginia Convention: the Independence Resolution of May 15, the Declaration of Rights of June 12, and the Virginia Constitution of June 29. The event serves as a poignant reminder of the oratorical achievements of Patrick Henry and Thomas Jefferson, who, among others, contributed richly to the American heritage and tradition during the eighty-one years that Williamsburg was the capital of the Virginia Colony.

In his address Mr. Webb linked the theme of individual liberty with our intellectual capacity to reach out beyond the rims of the earth's surface:

> The men who labored here [Williamsburg] in 1776 took the long view of man: man in space, if you will, since to the best of their knowledge—and ours—man has always been in space and always will be. He was in space when King John at Runnymede made his giant step toward guaranteed human rights.

Man will be in space when, in the foreseeable future, he projects himself to the moon or even more distant moons—perhaps to Ganymede, the little-known moon that revolves around Jupiter. The challenge at Williamsburg, said Mr. Webb:

was to establish an *independent order of free and responsible men* whose physical frontier would then move north, south, and west, but whose intellectual expansion would be bounded solely by their individual capacities and their ability to cooperate. This challenge was met so magnificently that the physical frontier is not now measured in the horizontal but by the vertical—it is out in space away from earth. We are exploring this frontier with Mariner and Surveyor, and also with Glenn and Schirra, as Jefferson probed north and west with Lewis and Clark. Today's frontier is limited only by our ability to maintain individual freedom and yet join many minds and hands in concerted action. Independence must continue to find a way to include interdependence in spite of complexity. Interdependence is the root of the nonlinearity which marks the safe limits of our over-all systems and of our individual lives.

It is a great honor to share with you the privilege of meeting here in Williamsburg to recall the concepts of individual liberty, self-government, responsible leadership, and public service breathed into life by the great American patriots who did their work here in the fifty days from May 15 to July 4, 1776. Time and again on these occasions Governor Winthrop Rockefeller and his distinguished guests have pointed out that independence for the United States was accomplished because the leaders of Virginia based their work on a deep understanding of man as an individual and as a collection of individuals making up society.

While the main events that we commemorate here today took place in fifty days, there was a long period in which, to use Woodrow Wilson's words,

the great continent lay "a veiled and virgin shore" inflaming desires that could not be gratified, stirring dreams that only enticed brave men to their death, exciting to enterprise and adventure, but never to substantial or lasting achievement.

Then came a colonial development prelude that lasted more than fifty years. Even the Byrds of Virginia had to submit to the rigors of this period. In fact, in 1717, having lost his first wife, William Byrd of Westover was in London paying ardent suit to a young lady named Mary Smith whose father required that he set down an analysis of his property and income. He did this, adding a statement of his honorable descent from the Byrds of Cheshire. But Mr. Smith replied coldly that property on the moon was as acceptable as an estate in Virginia. So Byrd lost Mary Smith.

Today, the moon seems much nearer, and samples of it are eagerly awaited by scientists all over the world. It is nearer because over 400,000 men and women have worked hard to develop every scientific discipline, every major area of technology, and every engineering and management requirement to succeed in the largest and most complex non-military undertaking of all time. Our nation has mobilized for this project within a decade about the same number of people required to build our transcontinental railroads. As independent individuals, these people have cooperated to use gravity, inertia, thermodynamics, and celestial mechanics in extraordinary new ways. They have constructed a rocket-powered transportation system that is already being used again and again, not only to the moon, but to almost any place in the solar system.

Property from the moon will soon become a more acceptable asset than even an estate in Virginia. Today, communications satellites and weather satellites are serving to tie the peoples of Europe, Asia, North America, and Australia together and to provide to the entire world useful weather information.

On June 25 [1967], the people of twenty-four nations, completely girdling the earth, will simultaneously watch the same television program—which will tell millions of men what other men are doing at many, many points around the world. It is an interesting fact that communications satellites of both the United States and the Soviet Union will make this possible.

Thirty-nine nations currently receive cloud-cover pictures on a routine basis from our weather satellites.

During the period from February to April, a combination of surface-based, airborne, seaborne, and satellite observations were taken in the Pacific which will be used to study fundamental meteorological problems.

Observing the earth from satellites will soon provide a powerful means for us and other nations to locate potential areas of mineral and oil resources.

Man is not only looking toward how space can serve him here on earth, but is also continuing to look further outward into space, eagerly awaiting the time when he can travel to the moons of planets other than his own earth. One such moon revolves around Jupiter, that distant and little-known planet. Its name is Ganymede, and it was discovered by Galileo 150 years before the famous fifty days we celebrate here today.

The capability man now has to project himself or his instruments to our own nearby moon or a distant moon of Jupiter is, of course, dependent on that developed intellectuality which flourishes on man's independence nourished by individual liberty, and freedom of choice. This is less well stated in our history books than is the story of that great turning point in man's struggle for independence and liberty that occurred at Runnymede in the thirteenth century. Runnymede means to most of us an epoch in man's struggle for his natural rights and for self-fulfillment. Ganymede means an intellectual concept and an object so distant that we can hardly reach it in this century. But both are symbolic. Therefore, I have chosen for my topic today, "From Runnymede to Ganymede."

The men who labored here in 1776 took the long view of man: man in space, if you will, since to the best of their knowledge—and ours—man has always been in space and always will be. He was in space when King John at Runnymede made his giant step toward guaranteed human rights. He was in space at Padua in the seventeenth century when Galileo Galilei made his giant step toward understanding his place in space with the aid of free scientific thought. And he will be in space at Ganymede in the twenty-first century if he chooses to stop there to do a detailed spectroanalysis of Jupiter to see if life exists. (This is an important concept because no one has yet figured out a way to land on Jupiter itself. Already, here on earth, we are performing experiments which show the possibility that some life could evolve even on that hostile planet.)

Thus, while this century will bring us the capability to travel to our moon and the nearby planets, Venus and Mars, man already begins to dream of going on to the distant planets in the next century. If Jefferson were alive today, he would without doubt be an enthusiastic participant in this thought process. In Jefferson there was a happy marriage of physical science and political science. Through him both were joined for good at Williamsburg in 1776.

Jefferson knew about Runnymede, and he was deeply committed to extend the progress man had made in the intervening five centuries. Interestingly enough, Jefferson also knew about Ganymede. More than this, he understood the profound importance of the interaction between the physical and the social sciences. He knew the sequence that plays itself out as man's attention is drawn to a phenomenon of nature and begins to think about it, to refine his observations, and to analyze them in depth. He understood that given enough motivation, enough intelligence, and enough time, man would then begin to identify the important elements and to perceive their relationships one to another. Jefferson recognized that through this scientific method there would come understanding, and that with sufficient understanding man could achieve the power to make predictions about the phenomenon to which his attention had been drawn.

Many who explain science and interpret the scientific method today stop at this point. But Jefferson, a close student of Bacon, recognized that with a deeper and more profound understanding, man discovers the basic principles that enable him to predict related phenomena, and that in time he will discover he can control some of these and put them to work.

The term we use today for man's ability to capture and put to work the forces of nature is "technology." Since technology frequently gives birth to better means for making new scientific observations, it continually provides the beginning of a whole new cycle of discovery, understanding, and practical use of knowledge.

As Jefferson thought deeply on the lessons of history in the spring of 1776, it seems to me hardly possible that he did not reflect on the fact that the most dramatic examples of man's scientific success had derived from his centuries-old interest in the vast regions outward from the earth. Jefferson was aware, for example, that almost two hundred years earlier, the famous Danish astronomer, Tycho Brahe, and his collaborators perfected the quadrant and made a long and especially accurate series of observations of the motions of the stars and planets. He was aware that a short time later Galileo Galilei applied the telescope to the more detailed study of our moon and the planets of our solar system. He knew that the observations of Brahe and Galileo cast great doubt on the then current theory which placed the earth at the center of the solar system and which had been man's egocentric view since the time of the ancient Greeks. Jefferson also knew that Johannes Kepler, a student of Brahe's, had achieved greatness by analyzing Brahe's data in detail and deducing his famous laws of planetary motion. And Jefferson knew well that Newton, who was described as "he who in genius surpassed human kind," had surveyed the work of Kepler on planetary motions and of Galileo on falling bodies and had concluded that the dynamics of these phenomena were really but manifestations of a universal principle which became his law of gravitation. Jefferson knew that Newton had gone on to enunciate his three famous laws of motion, and had become thereby, apart from relativistic considerations, the architect of dynamics and celestial mechanics as we know them today.

Here in Williamsburg two hundred years ago, Jefferson undoubtedly pondered the massive impact on man and society of this sequence of events. What did it mean, what could it mean to the new nation being born, that those literary and religious positions which had rallied around the fallacious earth-centered universe of Ptolemy, and were made vivid in the epic poems of Milton and Dante, had been so recently and so sorely shaken by advancing intellectual processes?

Could Jefferson have foreseen that man's lesson in humility and objectivity in the face of such a vast unfolding physical universe had only begun, and that the forces of a free-thinking science would shortly bring man to conceive that the solar system itself was nowhere near the center of the universe? Indeed, that the universe itself is an immense space-time continuum in which energy and mass are interchanging on a grand scale?

We know today that if knowledge is to be of benefit to mankind, it must be put to work through organized society. Jefferson knew this, too. He had read John Locke, and had placed his picture in his home. Indeed he had made Locke's *Essay Concerning Human Understanding* a subject of careful study. He knew what Galileo's great accomplishment had contributed to Newton's work and that it had also provided an inspirational basis for Newton's friend, Locke, in the fields of philosophy and government. The effect of Locke's works defining and defending human rights were strongly reflected in the Declaration of Independence and in much that came thereafter.

And so, it is today hard to imagine a grander consequence of the cross-fertilization of ideas in the history of man than that represented by Locke and Newton, as seen by Jefferson.

In our early days Washington, Hamilton, Jefferson, and Franklin built in concert on the knowledge of each other, and they did this with all the effectiveness that characterized the work of Brahe, Galileo, Kepler, and Newton. This was no small feat. Washington, the soldier, had to know government as he knew war; Hamilton, the lawyer, had to know banking as he knew jurisprudence; Jefferson, the philosopher, had to know men as he knew logic; and Franklin, the scientist, had to know diplomacy as well as he knew electricity. There was no assumption underlying their work more important than that individually free men would become collectively responsible men. They set a pattern of collective action and governmental framework that has enabled a growing society of free men to effectively exercise initiative in exploiting new knowledge through new technology on a scale never before attained. Our free society has become a select haven for free-thinking science and advanced technology, with the result that its search for and application of new knowledge has been successful on a scale that challenges all the rest of mankind.

But let us return to Newton and recall that his third law of motion, equating action and reaction, is especially suited for providing vehicles that move in the vacuum outside our atmosphere. This possibility was recognized by Robert Goddard, who conceived and developed the first small liquid rocket over thirty years ago. He laid the foundation for today's large space boosters that have already succeeded in taking man far away from the earth, where he may make even more revealing observations and find new ways to make use of his environment.

Truly, then, we are witnessing the full measure of John Wesley Powell's penetrating observation in 1888 when, as president of the American Association for the Advancement of Science, he stated,

In man's progress from savagery to enlightenment, he has transferred the laws of beast evolution from himself to his inventions, and relieved of the load, he has soared away to the goal of his destiny on the wings of higher law.

It may be instructive to mentally blast off from earth and look at ourselves as an *entity in the totality of this space region which we can now traverse.* Either individually or collectively as an element of mass or energy, man's presence in space can easily be calculated to be of trivial significance. On the grand scale of space, man appears to be a physical triviality.

As an intellectual entity, however, he is as uniquely significant in the totality of space as he is in the locality of earth. By all odds his destiny appears to be the destiny of his intellect. He appears to have no recourse but to engage by all means available in the endless search for new food for thought—new information which he digests to form the new knowledge that enables him to continue the search for better understanding of himself and of his environment.

This search then is the greatest continuing adventure known to man, and it is uniquely his in the physical universe. It is uniquely suited to constructively consuming all of his resources, mental and physical. Thus, if man so chooses, he does indeed have an outlet for all the effort now expended in conflict or wars, an outlet vastly more noble and rewarding.

But the events of the day make it clear that the existence of conflict and of war still provides dramatic evidence of the animal that remains in man; that man himself is the one animal that man has far from fully mastered.

George Mason penned in Article XV of the Virginia Declaration of Rights, "That no free government, or the blessing of liberty can be preserved to any people but by . . . frequent recurrence to fundamental principles."

What then are these principles as they apply today? To get at this question, let us take another view of ourselves, paying special attention to the impact of science and technology. It is important to note first that we have become a nation composed largely of specialists, both as individuals and as professional groups. This has been necessary in order to cope with the increasing number and complexity of the functions which must be performed, each of which must be tractable for the individual, for his professional or associated group, and for those who must fit them together to provide an effective total operation of society. In a very real sense, then, we have evolved into a highly complex, interconnected, and interdependent system of people, groups, functions, and interests. This is in contradistinction to our early period when the advancing frontier provided opportunity and fluidity, and the pattern of settlement consisted of a relatively small number of loosely connected groups which could enjoy a quasi-independent existence.

Now perhaps the most remarkable thing about this evolution is that our fundamental principles and rules of law and order have been able to adjust and to evolve at more or less the same rate. Within our constitutional frame of government this has served to preserve the essential independence and freedom of the individual and to maintain a balance of forces and positions between existing and new groups.

Increasingly, science and technology have been important forcing functions of this evolution. It is the prime purpose of science to enlarge our understanding of known phenomena and to begin our understanding of new phenomena. The output of this effort is new knowledge, which is put to work in improving the way we do things we already know how to do and in developing ways of doing things we never knew how to do before. Accordingly, science and technology facilitate the development of new and improved functions in our society, and the most effective management techniques for exploiting these functions have largely involved the specializing of peoples and groups.

More generally, however, the essential product of science and technology is *change*—that is, *change in the attitudes and interests of people* through the acquisition of new knowledge, and *change in the methods of action and interaction of people* through the application of this knowledge. It follows that the larger the effort in science and technology, the larger those changes will be and the more rapidly they will occur.

Is this sufficient background against which to ask if we today are participating in a prelude to independence or the loss of it in the twenty-first century? Can we now grasp the basic problem posed for the individual by big science and big technology as major continuing elements in the same way the problems of 1776 were grasped by the men we honor today?

We know that the effect of science and technology is to upset the dynamic equilibrium of society. The bigger the effort of science and technology, the bigger and more rapid these perturbations are likely to be.

The hard fact of life for organized society and its leaders today is that if dynamic equilibrium is achieved at any one time it becomes increasingly difficult to maintain. This is especially true when it is upset by a number of large innovations not introduced with the most careful consideration of their second- and third-order effects.

We have now, also, significant evidence that new and improved methods must be brought into play to analyze and prepare for the introduction of major innovations. These methods must include not only consideration of the direct benefits which the innovations are primarily intended to provide, but also the intellectual response-time of humans, the inertia of human systems, and the interaction of human endeavors with their supporting physical and social environment.

In the National Aeronautics and Space Administration our experience to date indicates that for success we must make the most careful analysis of all factors at the start and still be prepared to adjust to meet reality when conditions turn out to differ from those that were foreseen. When we proceed this way the "integrated systems" approach developed for defense systems and for space exploration is vastly more effective for specific purposes than the "independent components" approach to the solution of problems in complex dynamic systems.

We all know, I believe, that goals for society and the projects to achieve them are realistic only as they are achievable with existing systems or desirable modifications of such systems.

This means that goals, projects, and systems must, in the last analysis, be viewed as interdependent elements, and goals that depend on undesirable systems are undesirable goals. Cooperation is desirable; loss of independence or individuality is not. The classic and continuing goal of our society is to preserve those basic freedoms and rights that have been won for responsible individuals, and the essential bases for cooperation between responsible groups within the framework of representative government.

The problem of choosing goals in our society depends on both our capabilities and our desires. From a capability point of view, we have long since passed the stage of surviving in our natural environment. To be sure we are creating problems of environmental pollution, but these are in no sense intractable to scientific and technological solution. We are in the process of pulling up the rearward displaced elements of our society, and we are extending assistance to provide security and opportunity to many other peoples throughout the world. All of this we are doing, and yet there is still capability left over. Some desire is left over, too, and we are satisfying this desire by applying some of our remaining capability to the enlargement of our science and technology effort, on earth and out in space. Many important factors contribute to this, but there is one that stands out. This is the fact that the carefully conceived methods of science and technology provide the only proven means known to man for consistently enlarging and applying his understanding of himself and his environment. Moreover, man alone of all creatures has learned to develop and use these methods for these means.

In this setting, the opening of the space regions to man's exploration and use is an epoch of vast significance. It is a prelude to a new and endless quest for enlarging and applying our understanding of ourselves and our environment. It is uniquely our quest—our unique destiny, and our unlimited adventure.

And so, we arrive back at the starting point of the evolution of our free society from eighteenth-century Willamsburg toward an unknown but beckoning twenty-first century. The challenge at Williamsburg was to establish an *in-dependent order of free and responsible men* whose physical frontier would then move north, south, and west, but whose intellectual expansion would be bounded solely by their individual capacities and their ability to cooperate. This challenge was met so magnificently that the physical frontier is not now measured in the horizontal but by the vertical—it is out in space away from earth. We are exploring this frontier with Mariner and Surveyor, and also with Glenn and Schirra, as Jefferson probed north and west with Lewis and Clark. Today's frontier is limited only by our ability to maintain individual freedom and yet join many minds and hands in concerted action. Independence must continue to find a way to include interdependence in spite of complexity. Interdependence is the root of the nonlinearity which marks the safe limits of our over-all systems and of our individual lives.

Can we as individuals be *essentially free and yet inter-dependent?* This is Zeno's paradox of the twentieth century and it may continue into the twenty-first. Can we remain free and still put a governor on society that will stop us short of war? Can we remain independent and still go to Ganymede? How we answer it today and tomorrow will make up the character of any prelude to independence for man in the twenty-first century.

Much of what we can contribute to the answer lies in a fact that is obvious. This fact is the essential requirement for each of us to do what we can as individuals and as groups to make our system of representative government work, and then work better. More and more this means that each of us must find a way to reach through complexity and organized prejudice to organized facts and trusted sources of information. We must not do less than to make sure we understand the *fundamentals in the many important disciplines* of human activity.

Without this understanding of at least the fundamentals, from the golden rule to the laws of gravity and natural selection, today's citizen will not play the role only he can play in representative society, cannot bridge the gap from one discipline to another, from the old to the new. Without this, a citizen today cannot be a fully effective participant in a free society. Indeed, without this basic understanding on a large scale at all levels our nation is likely to forfeit the capability of collectively responsible action, and thus the opportunity and capability for an effective free society.

This is the heritage of the tremendous intellectual and cooperative effort made here in Williamsburg in the fifty days that were the prelude to independence in 1776. If we can now build on this heritage to achieve the same kind of success in the face of the massive complexities of our times, I am confident that free men of the twenty-first century will look as well upon us as we do upon the men whom we honor here today.

APPENDIX

BIOGRAPHICAL NOTES

BOORSTIN, DANIEL J. (1914-). Born, Atlanta, Georgia; A.B., Harvard University, 1934; B.A., first class honors, Rhodes scholar, Balliol College, Oxford University, 1936; B.C.L., 1937; J.S.D., Yale University, 1940; admitted, barrister-at-law, Inner Temple, 1937; instructor, history and literature, Harvard and Radcliffe, 1938-42; lecturer, legal history, Harvard Law School, 1939-42; admitted to Massachusetts bar, 1942; assistant professor of history, Swarthmore College, 1942-44; assistant professor of history, University of Chicago, 1944-49; associate professor, 1949-56; professor, 1956- ; lecturer for United States Department of State in Iran, India, Nepal, and elsewhere, 1959-60; Phi Beta Kappa; author, *The Mysterious Science of the Law*, 1941; *The Lost World of Thomas Jefferson*, 1948; *The Genius of American Politics*, 1953; *The Americans: The Colonial Experience*, 1958; *America and the Image of Europe*, 1960; *The Image, or What Happened to the American Dream*, 1962; *The American Primer*, 1966; and other publications. (See also *Current Biography: September 1968*.)

DICKEY, JOHN SLOAN (1907-). Born, Lock Haven, Pennsylvania; A.B., Dartmouth College, 1929; LL.B., Harvard University, 1932; admitted to Massachusetts bar, 1932; assistant to Commissioner, Massachusetts Department of Correction, 1933; in United States Department of State as legal adviser, 1934-36; in private law firm, 1936-40; public liaison officer, United States delegation, United Nations Conference on International Organization, San Francisco, 1945; president, Dartmouth College, 1945- ; originated Dartmouth "Great Issues" course. (See also *Current Biography: 1955*).

GALLAGHER, BUELL G. (1904-). Born, Rankin, Illinois; A.B., Carleton College, 1925; B.D., Union Theological Seminary, 1929; studied at London School of Economics, 1929-30; Ph.D., Columbia University, 1939; many honorary degrees, including ones from Oberlin College, Brandeis University, Columbia University, and

Carleton College; instructor, Doane College, 1925-26; ordained minister, Congregational Church, 1929; minister, Congregational Church, Passaic, New Jersey, 1931-33; president, Talladega College, 1933-34; professor of Christian ethics, Pacific School of Religion, 1944-49; director of Program Development, United States Office of Education, 1951; Assistant Commissioner of Education, 1951-52; president, The City College of New York, 1952-61; chancellor, California State College System, 1961-62; president, The City College of the City University of New York, 1962- ; actively associated with World University Service; Phi Beta Kappa; author, *Portrait of a Pilgrim: A Search for the Christian Way in Race Relations,* 1946; *Color and Conscience: The Irrepressible Conflict,* 1946. (See also *Current Biography: 1953.*)

GARDNER, JOHN W. (1912-). Born, Los Angeles, California; A.B. Stanford University, 1935; A.M., 1936; Ph.D., University of California, 1938; many honorary degrees, including LL.D., Brown University; University of Notre Dame, 1961; Hamilton College, 1962; teaching assistant, University of California, 1936-38; instructor in psychology, Connecticut College, 1938-40; assistant professor of psychology, Mt. Holyoke College, 1940-42; staff member, Carnegie Corporation, 1946-47; executive associate, 1947-49; vice president, 1949-55; president, 1955-65 (on leave) ; Secretary of Health, Education, and Welfare, 1965-68; head of The Urban Coalition, 1968- ; president, Foundation for the Advancement of Teaching; member, Woodrow Wilson Foundation, 1960-63; USMC, 1943-46; recipient, USAF Exceptional Services Award, 1956; author, *Excellence: Can We Be Equal and Excellent Too?* 1961; *Self-Renewal: The Individual and the Innovative Society,* 1964; *No Easy Victories,* 1968; editor, *To Turn the Tide,* 1962. (See also *Current Biography: 1956.*)

GAUD, WILLIAM STEEN (1907-). Born, New York City; A.B., Yale University, 1929; LL.B., 1931; editor of *Yale Law Review*; instructor, Yale Law School, 1931-33; with law firm, New York City, 1933-35; assistant corporation counsel, New York City, 1935-41; colonel, United States Army, World War II; special assistant to Secretary of War, 1945-46; member of law firm, New York City, 1961; deputy administrator of foreign aid agency; administrator, Agency for International Development, 1966- ; Legion of Merit with Oak Leaf Cluster; Order of British Empire.

GRISWOLD, ERWIN N. (1904-   ). Born, East Cleveland, Ohio; A.B., Oberlin College, 1925; A.M., 1925; LL.B., Harvard University Law School, 1928; many honorary degrees, including LL.D., Brown University, 1950; Columbia University, 1954; Northwestern University, 1960; University of Toronto, 1962; Princeton University, 1968; admitted to Ohio bar, 1929; admitted to Massachusetts bar, 1935; attorney, office of Solicitor General and special assistant to Attorney General, 1929-34; assistant professor of law, Harvard University Law School, 1934-35; professor, 1935-46; dean, 1950-67; Solicitor General of the United States, 1968-   ; member, United States Civil Rights Commission; member, Alien Enemy Hearing Board for Massachusetts, 1941-45; trustee, Oberlin College; president, Association of American Law Schools, 1957-58; fellow, American Academy of Arts and Sciences; Phi Beta Kappa; author, *Cases on Federal Taxation*, 1954; *The Fifth Amendment Today*, 1955; *Law and Lawyers in the United States*, 1964. (See also *Current Biography: 1956*.)

HOWE, HAROLD, II (1918-   ). Born, Hartford, Connecticut; A.B., Yale University, 1940; M.A., Columbia University, 1947; additional work, University of Cincinnati, 1953-57; Harvard University, 1960; LL.D., Princeton University, 1968; teacher, Darrow School, New Lebanon, New York, 1940-41; Phillips Academy, Andover, Massachusetts, 1947-50; principal, Andover Junior high school, 1950-53; Walnut Hills high school, Cincinnati, 1953-57; Newton (Massachusetts) high school, 1957-60; superintendent of schools, Scarsdale, New York, 1960-64; director, North Carolina Learning Institute, 1964-65; United States Commissioner of Education, 1965-   ; trustee, College Entrance Examination Board; served with USNR, 1941-45; trustee, Yale University; member, Commission on the Humanities. (See also *Current Biography: 1967*.)

JOHNSON, LYNDON BAINES (1908-   ). Born near Stonewall, Texas; graduate, Johnson City (Texas) high school, 1924; B.S., Southwest State Teachers College, San Marcos, Texas, 1930; student, Georgetown University Law School, 1935-36; teacher, public schools, Houston, Texas, 1930-32; secretary to Representative Richard M. Kleberg, 1932-35; state director, National Youth Administration for Texas, 1935-37; member, United States House of Representatives (Democrat, Texas), 1937-49; United States Senate, 1949-61; minority leader, 83rd Congress; majority leader, 84th-86th Congresses; resigned from United States Senate, January 3, 1961; Vice President of the United States, 1961-63; became President of the United States upon the assassination of President John F. Kennedy, November 22, 1963; elected President of the United States, 1964; author, *My Hope for America*, 1964. (See also *Current Biography: 1964*.)

KENNEDY, EDWARD M. (1932-   ). Born, Brookline, Massachusetts; A.B., Harvard University, 1954; LL.B., University of Virginia, 1959; United States Senate (Democrat, Massachusetts), 1962-   ; president, Joseph P. Kennedy, Jr. Foundation, 1961-   ; member, board of trustees, Boston University; Lahey Clinic; member, Senate Committee on the Judiciary; Committee on Labor and Public Welfare; author, *Decisions for a Decade*, 1968. (See also *Current Biography: 1963*.)

KERR, CLARK (1911-   ). Born, Stony Creek, Pennsylvania; A.B., Swarthmore College, 1932; M.A. Stanford University, 1933; student, London School of Economics, 1936, 1939; Ph.D., University of California, 1939; many honorary degrees, including LL.D., Harvard University, 1958; Princeton University, 1959; instructor of economics, Antioch College, 1936-37; teaching fellow, University of California, 1937-38; assistant and associate professor, University of Washington, 1940-45; associate professor and professor, University of California, 1945-52; director, Institute of Industrial Relations, University of California, 1945-52; chancellor, University of California, 1952-58; president, 1958-67; chairman, Carnegie Foundation Commission on the Future of Higher Education, 1967-   ; extensive service in labor arbitration; National Wage Stabilization Board, 1950-51; member, War Labor Board, 1943-45; vice chairman, American Council on Education, 1953-54; board of directors, Center for Advanced Study in Behavioral Science, 1953-61; Phi Beta Kappa; author or co-author, *Unions, Management and the Public* 1948, 1960; *Industrialism and Industrial Management*, 1960; *The Uses of the University*, 1963. (See also *Current Biography: 1961*.)

LINDSAY, JOHN V. (1921-   ). Born, New York City. A.B., Yale University, 1944; LL.B., 1948; admitted to New York bar, 1949; partner in law firm, New York City, 1953-66; executive assistant to United States Attorney General, 1955-57; United States House of Representatives (Republican, New York), 1959-65; mayor, City of

New York, 1966- ; USNR, 1943-46; president, New York Republican Club, 1952; member, board of trustees, Freedom House; author, *Journey into Politics,* 1967. (See also *Current Biography: 1962.*)

MANSFIELD, MICHAEL JOSEPH (1903-). Born, New York City; student, Montana School of Mines, 1927-28; A.B., Montana State University, 1933; A.M., 1934; student, University of California, 1936, 1937; United States Navy, 1918-19; United States Army, 1919-20; United States Marines, 1920-22; in mining engineering, 1922-31; professor of history and political science, Montana State University, 1933-42; United States House of Representatives (Democrat, Montana), 1943-52; United States Senate, 1953- ; majority leader, 1961- ; member, Senate Foreign Relations Committee; Committee on Appropriations; member, various delegations to Asia and Europe, including Southeast Asia Conference, Manila, 1954. (See also *Current Biography: 1952.*)

MAYS, BENJAMIN E. (1895-). Born, Epworth, South Carolina; A.B., Bates College, 1920; M.A., University of Chicago, 1925; Ph.D., 1935; many honorary degrees, including D.D., Howard University, 1945; Bates College, 1947; Bucknell University, 1954; L.H.D., Boston University, 1950; New York University, 1968; instructor, Morehouse College, 1921-24; professor of English, State College of South Carolina, Orangeburg, 1925-26; executive secretary, Urban League in Tampa, 1926-28; dean, School of Religion, Howard University, 1934-40; president and president emeritus, Morehouse College, 1940- ; delegate to World Council of Churches, 1948, 1954; recipient, Christian Culture Award, Assumption University, Windsor, Ontario, Canada; Phi Beta Kappa; Delta Sigma Rho; author, *The Christian in Race Relations,* 1954; compiler, *A Gospel for the Social Awakening,* 1950; and other publications.

UDALL, MORRIS K. (1922-). Born, St. Johns, Arizona; LL.B., University of Arizona, 1949; admitted to Arizona bar, 1949; partner in law firm, 1949-61; county attorney, Pima County, Arizona, 1953-54; United States House of Representatives (Democrat, Arizona), 1961- ; member, House Committee on Interior and Insular Affairs; Committee on Post Office and Civil Service; captain USAAF, 1942-46; director, Bank of Tucson; trustee, Arizona-Sonora Desert Museum; author, *Arizona Law of Evidence,* 1960.

WEBB, JAMES E. (1906-). Born, Tally Ho, Granville County, North Carolina; A.B., University of North Carolina, 1928; student, George Washington University Law School, 1933-36; many honorary degrees, including LL.D., University of North Carolina, 1949; Sc.D., University of Notre Dame, 1961; with Sperry Gyroscope Corporation, 1936-43; executive assistant to Under Secretary of the Treasury, 1946; director, Bureau of the Budget, 1946-49; Under Secretary of State, 1949-52; deputy governor, International Bank for Reconstruction and Development, 1949-52; president, Republic Supply Company, 1953-58; assistant to president and director, Kerr-McGee Oil Industries, 1952-61; administrator, National Aeronautics and Space Administration, 1961-68; service with 1st Marine Air Warning Group, 1944-45; member, President's Committee on Manpower; President's Advisory Committee on Supersonic Transport; trustee, National Geographic Society; Phi Beta Kappa. (See also *Current Biography: 1962*.)

CUMULATIVE AUTHOR INDEX

1960-1961—1967-1968

A cumulative author index to the volumes of REPRESENTATIVE AMERICAN SPEECHES for the years 1937-1938 through 1959-1960 appears in the 1959-1960 volume.